Synchronicity

(What are the chances?)

By

*Wishing you many happy coincidences!
love
Tamasin Blake*

Tamasin F. Blake

Copyright © 2023 Tamasin F. Blake

All rights reserved.

ISBN:
ISBN 9781973233961

There is more to life than the human eye can see. This book is dedicated to everyone who feels alone, lost, or generally mystified about what they are doing on the planet.

Know that you are not alone.

For my dear brother Robert (Bob)
1960 – 1976 (death by suicide)

Contents

Introduction	5
Chapter I Who, What, Where, When, Why and How	9
Chapter II Categories of Coincidence	65
Chapter III Anti-Synchronicity	65
Chapter IV Synchronicity Journal	65
Chapter V Symbolism Meanings	65
My final coincidence story	65
Chapter VI Curiouser and Curiouser (Otherwise known as Full Woo)	65
Bibliography	65

Introduction

Hello Dear Reader,

A TRIGGER warning about this book. It does have references to suicide and death. This warning is meant to serve as a STOP READING point for anyone who doesn't want to read about people who end their life early. So, dear reader, consider yourself warned.

I love synchronicity and I am long enough in the snaggle-tooth not to give a flying fig what other people think, but still, it is quite high risk to declare that you believe in things that you cannot see and you can't really explain. Most coincidence stories bring a feeling of upliftment, hope and happiness, but not all of them. I am sorry if any of my stories evoke feelings of sadness or pain, it isn't my intention to bring down a vibe, but this is life, right?

Some life events are miserable, unpleasant, unwanted and sad, it is all part of the rich tapestry of our life experience. I am grateful to synchronicity because it has kept me going through some tough times in my life.

I am sharing my experiences, my understanding and my beliefs, in an attempt to help other people who might also find themselves in need of spiritual sustenance and hope. Hope that life does have meaning and everything does matter. It is difficult to convey how meaningful the coincidences are without explaining some backstory. I didn't set out to tell my own life story against the backdrop of coincidence, so I have tried to keep the backstories to as much of a minimum as I could whilst maintaining the integrity of the story.

I have loved synchronicity since around 1986. Thirty years passed before this book started coming into being. This little collection of stories took around two years of sporadic note-taking, followed by three years of procrastination. My aim here, dear lovely reader, is to encourage you to create a record of your own synchronicities, coincidences, high strangeness, and weird events that happen in your own life so when you look back, you will be able to recall them easily and perhaps spot your own life patterns as they unfold in front of you.

I have chosen this moment to put this little book out to the Universe because of a 'sign'. A literal sign. This 'sign story' makes up my final offering for this book. The synchronicity that showed up for me, which I chose to interpret as a sign that it is time for me to stop adding information to this book, time to stop increasing my coincidence journal and publish it, is at the end of my synchronicity journal in Chapter IV.

Forgive me, dear reader, if I have used annoying phrases or committed crimes of grammar, font, or print. I have not set out to upset anyone by using undesirable phrases, cliches, predictable words, or whatever irks your well-being. These words have been written with love in mind. I have paid attention to the Universe with a sense of wonder and awe of this life we are living, and I do have a deep appreciation of the synchronicities that have shown up as I have written this book, or maybe they have shown up because I am writing this book. The mystery of coincidence is a beautiful part of life experience to be enjoyed and shared. It is in this spirit of love, awe, light and laughter that I share my observations, both personal coincidence stories, as well as some stories I have heard on my travels from friends and strangers alike.

I have also created meanings for the signs and events, which I have listed in Chapter V of this book. I am happy for you to look at the meanings that I have attributed to the items that have shown up on my life path, both in the form of inanimate objects and life events. Whether you wish to interpret your coincidences the same way that I have, is your choice. If the meaning I have given feels right to you, then trust your inner knowing. Trusting your intuition is essential to interpreting coincidence, like interpreting dreams. It is your understanding of what the sign means that really matters.

Sometimes the signs show up and have no meaning at all. I love those coincidences as well! I thank the Universe, thank Source, thank God, or whatever term you feel comfortable applying to a Higher Intelligence/source of consciousness and creator of synchronicity within which we live.

I love coincidence so much that I have kept a journal, taken photos and regularly shared my experience on Instagram @taztasticsilver. Enjoy my musings, dear reader, and please do feel free to share your coincidence stories with me www.tamasinblake.com

Chapter I

Who, what, where, when, why and how

"Meaningful coincidence of two or more events where something other than the probability of chance is involved."

Carl Jung

There is no such thing as Coincidence. Coincidences do not happen by accident. It is not a coincidence that you are reading this book. The Universe has brought you to this point. Where to begin?

Well, who, what, where, when, why and how of coincidence, I will start there. The Five W's and H. These are the questions surrounding any good story. This is how I have tried to sort out and sift through the information currently available to me about synchronicity. In this situation I think it makes more sense to start with the 'What', so I have committed some sort of literary crime and swapped 'Who' with 'What'.

What?

What is synchronicity? No-one knows. Next!

All synchronicity is a calling card from a higher intelligence. Synchronicity is as difficult to describe as it is to understand. What is synchronicity? Well, I can offer you some sets of ideas by way of explanation, but generally, the whole of this book tries to answer that question.

It is information so heightened as for us humans to call it a coincidence. Sometimes the events/information are so deliciously improbable, unlikely and unexplainable we call it synchronicity. The timing is perfect, the data is succinct and it has deep meaning for the person in the middle of it.

Synchronicity is a set of acausal events which often leave us with our mouths open. 'Did you see what just happened?' 'You will never believe it, but…' with a story to tell which is often repeated through the years to demonstrate the unexplainable. Not everything is easily explained.

Synchronicity inspires us with awe. Synchronicity is when events line up which transcend mere coincidence and we are left shaking our heads, mystified about what just happened. I believe that synchronicity is evidence of a higher intelligence at work. The Universe delivers up the extraordinary and often perplexing interplay of events that defy all odds and prompts us to ask 'What are the chances?' 'What are the odds?'.

It is all in the timing of the events. This is all part of the mystery. How did that happen right at that moment, right then, right at that exact moment? How do all these events and circumstances come together at exactly that precise moment? The exact day, the hour, the minute, and sometimes the precise second to have meaning for the person who is witnessing the coincidence.

I believe that Synchronicity is a gift from the Universe, a beautiful, clever, intelligent delivery of a message from our friends in Spirit to either wake us up or remind us of their presence around us. Synchronicity is a form of communication from Spirit to us little earthbound peeps.

Coincidence is a gift of information, knowledge and power. Clues are all around us for which directions to take, who to speak to, who to go into business with, which firm to work for, what sort of work to do. If ever you need help accessing this information Ask the Universe.

Who?

Who experiences coincidence? Who does synchronicity show up for? People who have an interest in synchronicity and coincidence. Not necessarily people who are looking for coincidence, but people who have a mindset that is able to recognise life events, symbols, creatures, nature and the people around them. People who are switched on. People who know that there is meaning to life, are more likely to notice and to experience synchronicity. People who are aware of their own energy output.

There are many people on the planet who are having coincidental events and experiences which bring them comfort and feel so meaningful as to be life-changing for them and even for the people who are just hearing about the synchronicity are having their lives changed for the better.

Coincidence can, and does, happen for anyone. It is more likely to happen to people who are emotionally invested in a coincidental experience. The person who lives in joy and loves coincidence, may will notice more coincidences than a person who doesn't believe there is an intelligent Universe dishing up coincidences on our behalf.

Everyone can, however, some people seem to be more aware of coincidences than others. Sometimes even the most hard-headed, material bound person is slapped with a coincidence which they find difficult to just skip over, overlook or ignore. I think a lot of people are aware of coincidence and although some people attribute meaning (as I have done), to life events and symbolism, not everyone is left in awe at synchronicity, especially coincidences which happen to other people. Some people find it hard to empathise with a coincidence which has no meaning for them personally.

There is another train of thought that coincidence and synchronicity show up in the improbable life. The lives of the insecure, the unstable lives. Why would this be? Why would coincidence show up in the life of the superstitious, the weak, the schizophrenics, the poor, more than the wealthy, the strong, the secure? Again, how are we to know?

Not everyone admits to experiencing coincidence and they certainly don't admit to assigning any meaning to it. Not everyone admits to noticing signs and even fewer people would admit to acting on signs. We live in a society where Science is King, the rational mind is the only one to be listened to. There is only a very small place at the table for intuition, only the weak-willed would dream of believing in things they cannot see. I feel it is a fear, of 'What Other People Think' which prevents most people from 'coming out' about their beliefs in signs, portents, symbolism and messages from the Universe

Synchronicity shows up for a person who lives in the moment, for the moment, with no thought for the future, and who may well be creating their own instability. Or they may be creating their own reality. The person living with an open mind may be living in the middle of an unstable, unwritten life experience. A person with no definite goal, no set path, no direction, no definite purpose is at risk of allowing the Universe (which has a propensity towards Chaos) to take control and mess with them. It is this person who finds themselves at the mercy of divine intervention, in the form of a set of improbable circumstances, otherwise

known to us as Synchronicity. The Universe conspires to save his soul or perhaps even his life and to create a stable scenario around the person. I can imagine, it is easy if you try (said John Lennon) an intelligent Universe, rushing to his aid and bringing seemingly implausible events together, synchronicities which only a higher intelligence could possibly put together in order
to help him realise the path for his highest good. I also think that the coincidence stories which make it into common knowledge, mainly, are extreme. They have to be extreme to pique our interest, and when does a set of synchronicities become obvious? When it is extreme. An extreme set of disastrous circumstances would take an extreme set of synchronicities to save the person in the middle of it.

We will never know if the Universe dishes up more meaningful coincidences for people who keep the experiences to themselves. You know, like being generous and not telling people about it. Have you heard that one? If you are generous and you tell everyone what a generous person you are, then you are not that generous natured. If you need other people to know about your generosity, then the ulterior motive to your giving nature is just to be highly thought of by other people. Which sort of cancels out the acts of generosity. Your generosity ideally is between you and the person you have gifted with your generosity and God. I can't remember where I heard that little snippet from. I think it comes from some beliefs in Karma, the idea that what goes around comes around and if you tell people of your good works, you have already been rewarded.

I wonder if it is the same with coincidence. I risk sharing my coincidences because I am happy for people to think what they want of me. In order to put this information out there, as a way to help people, I have to accept that it might be met with ridicule and scorn. Which is okay by me. This book is for those who have eyes to see.

There is so much still that we don't know isn't there? Whatever your beliefs or your understanding or experience of Spiritual Laws, know that coincidence is right up there with the highest vibration in the Universe.

Back to the business of being bothered about what other people think. You know, believing in synchronicity as a communication from a higher intelligence and not wanting to talk with other people about it in case they think we are completely mad. It is no surprise that people keep their coincidences to themselves.

There is a reason for this, and for those of you who have tried to share your stories with people, you will have realized that not everyone can see anything special or meaningful about coincidences. Some people will even look at you as if you are 'cookie' or as if you are slightly crazy. Particularly if the experience has had a profound, deeply felt effect on you. If you accept this as a general situation in the 21st Century, that despite physicists and scientists uncovering previously unknown information every year, coincidence and synchronicity are dismissed as meaningless, for the simple-minded. Although, in fairness, a lot of these scientists also write God off in the same way.

So, know that you are not alone, the Universe brought the coincidence to you. The coincidences are between you and the Universe and if you don't want to share them with anyone else, that is totally fine. In order to share your coincidences, you do have to be thick-skinned enough to be able to take some criticism, or at least to be able to brush off the criticism, knowing that if people aren't ready to enjoy your coincidences with you, it is their loss.

In this strange Universe, we don't even know if our thoughts affect other people, or if thoughts are contagious, in any way, and yet we are often still so concerned with what other people are going to think of us that we can't speak up about what we do believe. As a therapist, I have spent many hours sitting with people who have been virtually paralysed, mentally and emotionally from physically acting in their own lives because of fear of what other people are going to think. Either a fear of judgement, or a fear of loss of status or reputation in the eyes of other people.

After working through these thoughts, it can be easy to accept the idea that you don't know what other people are going to think. It can take some practice to learn how to 'leave their thinking with them'. Leave it with the Other Person. If you can learn to do that, it does help enormously. I know it is more complicated than to think 'If they don't pay your bills, is it any of their business', but this is a good start. If another person sees us as a person who believes in a Higher Power, they might change their view of us, they might reject us, they might treat us differently, or have less respect for us as people. These are all fears which can become a reality and not everyone is fortunate enough to be able to be so independent as to not be bothered about other people's thinking. Which is sad, but also, seems to be creating a society where people are scared to make any moves through fear of the response of the crowd, which may be real or imaginary!

Dear reader, allow me to interrupt this flow with a story. A recent experience I had of someone who was scared to tell people she was visiting a Law of Attraction Seminar. My little trip to Amsterdam in 2023 led me to meeting some lovely people. One lady had lied to her relatives about where she was going, purely because she was so concerned with what they would think of her, and she didn't want to have to deal with their negativity and protestations about what she was doing.

Fortunately for me, I am in a stage of my life where I am less dependent on the opinion of others, not completely independent but I only have a few years before retirement, so if the worse comes to the worst I will only have a few lean years!

I am also very fortunate to have developed a secure sense of my inner being, my sense of self is not that easy to shake – hoorah! But, for those of you still on your journey of being dependent/semi-dependent/co-dependent on the opinion of others, I can completely understand why you would want to keep your amazing synchronicity stories to yourself. If a story only has deep meaning for you, not everyone is going to 'get it'. Not everyone is going to understand why it feels so important to you.

Your work here is not to try and explain to people who don't have the ears to hear. That would be like talking about your feelings to someone who is non-empathic. Or like banging your head against a brick wall. Pointless, discouraging and disheartening and it might even deter you from sharing your feelings again. If you are blessed enough to be touched by meaningful coincidence, it is your choice whether you share that story with other people.

There is no way of telling how people are going to react, and if you are in any way uncertain of how they will feel about it, then it is probably best to keep your story to yourself until you feel completely comfortable to share it. Or until you are sure that you can handle any fallout, criticism, push-back or attempted invalidation of your feelings. Or as the Bible quote says 'do not cast pearls before swine'.

In the King James Version of the Bible, Mathew 7:6 states, "Give not that which is holy unto the dog, neither cast ye your pearls before swine lest they trample them under their feet and turn again and rend you". In other words, don't give things of value to those who will not understand or appreciate them.

I think it can be a harsh life lesson to realise that not all information is meant for everyone. Sometimes it is not the right time for that person to have the information. Putting out feelers around certain subjects is always a good idea, rather than jumping in and laying it all out there for them to take it or leave it. Try not to waste your energy where possible. Sometimes it can't be helped, obviously, we can't get it right every time, but trusting your own intuition is a good place to start. The information you have been blessed with is between you and Source, or the Universe or God. It is your story. Share it with who you want.

Where?

Everywhere and anywhere. At home, at work, at school, college, in church, at the doctors, the vets, in the supermarket queue, indoors, outdoors, via the computer screen, your phone, on holiday, while you are asleep, in your dreams, while meditating, having a chat, at a party, on holiday, doing the housework. Literally, anywhere and everywhere.

Whether the territory is familiar or completely foreign to you, matters not. Sometimes the coincidences are noticed because we are paying more attention when we don't know which road we have to drive down or which bus we have to catch, so we are paying more attention to our surroundings, as a matter of necessity, but the coincidences can and do show up in our everyday habitat. Places often feature in coincidences, and sometimes just the place name.

Trip to Devon Story

Many years ago, I was living in Westliff-on-Sea, Essex in the UK. I was visiting my Mum who was living in Devon. A little back story for you, you know, because I can. If you can't be self-indulgent writing your own book, where can you be? The relationship between my Mum and I was strained and difficult for both of us.

We did manage to keep in contact, and we wrote each other letters, at least three times a week. At times in our lives this correspondence kept us both going, and it kept us in touch with the important things that were happening as well as the less important things.

Often, we wrote about tarot readings we had or messages from mediums in Spiritualist Churches.

Towards the end of her life, we had smoothed over a lot of our difficulties, and we had healed some of the most damaging aspects of our relationship. I would say that we had the best relationship that could have been expected from either of us.

There was no ill-will, nothing to be forgiven and a deep understanding and respect between us. We did have a good laugh whenever we spoke on the phone, because we did understand each other, and we could get on each other's wavelength with a little wiggle from either side. I would call it success that we had moved past the worst of our life experiences together and we were still communicating. To this end, of trying to stay in touch, I would visit her every couple of years. She had moved to Devon to retire, not just from work, but also from the trauma of her experiences in Essex. Moving away, for her, felt like a healing option.

As I was growing up, I picked up the habit of going to Spiritualist Church from my mum. My mum had a need to hear from my brother Robert, after he committed suicide at the tender age of 15 (I was 10 at the time). My mum had been to a medium who had told her that my brother was going by the name Bob now. In spirit, Bob. Bob in Spirit. We both took that on board, it seemed right to both of us that he would have gone from a Robert to a Bob.

Travelling 300 miles to visit my mum involved borrowing or hiring a car, saving money to pay for petrol from limited resources, just for perhaps a thirty-minute visit which was all my Mum could handle. It was a source of duty for both of us, we met up because we 'should', but it wasn't a natural desire from either of us.

This particular year, I had done my bit. I had arranged a car, petrol, my son had been looked after by a friend and I had made it to Devon for a couple of days. At the time I knew my brother in Spirit would have wanted me to carry on trying to have a relationship with my mum. I think it was harder for her to see me, than for me to see her, but she made the effort, and we managed the stress and anxiety between us. I think this is enough for you to know dear reader, by way of understanding how I was feeling about my trip to Devon.

By the second day we had both had enough of each other, even though we had some beautiful coincidences during the first day (I will come to that story in a moment, let me finish this part of the story first). I decided that I needed some space and air and I chose to take a walk on my own. My mum didn't want to venture out and definitely not to any unknown places. I looked around, pre-google, and decided to walk to the highest point in sight, the 'peak' of a nearby hill. I walked up the hill, stomping off my frustrations and some sadness, a lot of confusing emotions to deal with every time I met up with my mum.

Walking up the cobbled stones, I appreciated the beautiful architecture, the history of the buildings and I headed for the top. As I reached the top of the hill I appreciated the beautiful view of the sea, a perfect blue sky, a few white clouds, some seagulls cawing and a perfect snapshot for my mind. An optical reward for making the effort of climbing a hill. As I turned to head back down I noticed a plaque on the side of a house wall. It was the only house at the top of the hill. The house was called Westcliff. Which is where I had just driven from. It made me laugh. The Universe giving me something to laugh at amidst the sadness. It was perfect and I loved the coincidence. When I saw my mum the next day, it lightened her mood as well, we both enjoyed the coincidence.

Another synchronicity happened during that particular visit. My mum and I had agreed to walk along the promenade by the sea. A short walk, just to meet up and spend a little bit of time together. Literally a little bit of time.

We walked along the seafront heading towards a colourful marquee where there was a queue of people. Naturally curious over a queue, our British genes kicked in and my mum and I walked towards a grassy area. I had been talking to my mum about synchronicity and coincidence and what it means. I mentioned it because I had the name Ash had been showing up as I was walking to see my mum.

My son, Charlie, has a good friend, the son of one of my friends, his name is Ash and the name kept showing up. I was contemplating the idea that it isn't just people in Spirit who send nudges to say 'Hello', sometimes the Universe prompts us to contact people who are still living.

As my mum and I stood there, we watched as a line of donkeys were led past us towards the queue for some children to ride them up and down the beach. The beautiful little donkeys all had coloured nosebands with their names printed on them. The first donkey was called Ash. We both laughed and it was such a light relief moment, a reminder for both of us that laughter was such a big part of our relationship, it really did help to heal both of us because we had the same sense of humour.

The next little donkey walked past; his name was Charlie. We laughed again! Both the names that we had been talking about. The third donkey was called Rob! A reminder of my brother in Spirit. Neither of us laughed. I felt surprised.

The next donkey came along and the noseband read 'Pinky'. I didn't have anything meaningful around the name Pinky, but I was still enjoying the coincidence of the names of the first three donkeys. I glanced at my mum and she was holding her hand to her mouth. She seemed shocked. She held her hand out to show me her little finger, her pinky finger. She was wearing a pinky ring with a blue stone which I had never seen before, she explained that she wears it to remind her of Rob. For my Mum, the names of the last two donkeys had more meaning than a lot of tarot readings and church services put together.

We walked away from the donkeys, pleased, satisfied and surprised by the experience. I know I felt as though I had been touched by Spirit and that experience alone made the trip worthwhile. It was a very special moment and I am sure my Mum felt something similar.

Fleetwood Mac Story

When struggling Fleetwood Mac left Britain for LA, Christine's Mum, who was psychic, suggested they might find a miracle in an orange grove. On their first meeting in 1975, Stevie Nicks told Christine she lived on Orange Grove Avenue.

When?

The times synchronicities show up in our lives can be:

a) when we desperately need them to

b) when we ask for them

c) when we are alert to subtle events

d) randomly and entirely unexpectedly.

Coincidences can happen at any time, but I have found that they are more likely to happen at some times than others. The same way that some people are more sensitive to the phases of the moon than others, there are times when coincidences are more likely to happen than others.

Or more accurately, there are times when we are more able to perceive the event, data, sign or symbolism and interpret it as a coincidence. I have noticed that the seemingly very weird, extreme synchronicities show up when we are in a dire place in our life.

Synchronicity does seem to occur during times of instability. At times when there is a disaster about to happen, during a time of extreme stress and especially when the future is uncertain. Or maybe we are more likely to notice a series of fortunate events during a time of high drama.

Sometimes we can be happily plodding along, not expecting anything out of the ordinary and voila, there it is, just what we needed, as a strange coincidence to jolt us awake. A prod from the Universe. The Universe is asking us to wake up to the possibilities of events, happenings, and people, in our daily life. You never know what is coming around the corner and the Universe is full of infinite possibilities.

If you tune in to the Universe, the coincidences will flow your way more frequently with more meaning and you will wonder how you ever managed to ignore them! I daresay coincidence is an almost impossible subject to quantify, mainly because the act of looking at something, changes the thing being looked at. Is it possible that people who are expecting coincidences to happen are having more of them? I suspect that it is.

It seems as though the Universe does have a right time and a right place, there is a destiny unfolding. Although I have spent a lot of time studying astrology, I haven't found anything in astrology on a personal level in people's personalities which relates to their birth charts or death charts. I have tried.

The closest thing I have found is that many people do seem to have major changes during their Saturn return, which generally most people only have twice in a lifetime, some people live long enough for a third Saturn return and maybe as people will be living longer, they will have a third Saturn return to look forward to. You know the sort of change, the life review, taking stock of where you are, where you are going, perhaps a divorce is on the cards, a change of career, a move of house, a change of country, a baby, a commitment, sometimes a death of a close relative or parents often fall within Saturn Returns.

This question of 'when?' has also reminded me of a statement by Esther-hicks, (www.abraham-hicks.com) one of her mantras that she often uses: 'You can't get it wrong, and you never get it done'.

I think that statement is supposed to make you feel better. I guess by letting you off the hook. If that makes you feel better. Of course, it does let you off the hook, unless your emotional state is hovering somewhere around futility and then all it does is make you feel like there is no point in trying to achieve anything because there is always the next task to complete or goal to achieve. From a place of depression, this is just a reminder that life never ends, from a state of optimism this feels like there is always something to look forward to. It does just depend on your point of view.

I do believe that you can get it wrong. You can get it very, very, wrong and you can live with the consequences of being so mistaken. You can learn from getting it wrong. From a philosophical viewpoint, if you have learnt from it, then was it really a mistake? Or did you just have a costly life lesson?

If you hadn't made that bad choice, if you hadn't taken the inappropriate, not recommended, road, you would have missed that lesson/experience. If you learn from other people's mistakes, you can save yourself a lot of pain, but you do also miss the lessons and the satisfaction which comes from gaining your own life experience.

I wouldn't recommend life experience at all costs, but I can see how, from an extremely optimistic viewpoint, you can paint a positive narrative in order to be able to cope with the Truth of the matter. You may have made some humdinger mistakes, but they were your mistakes. You may never get it done, but would you want to? Would you really want to complete the Game of Life, leaving you free to absolutely nothing?!

Falling Baby Story

As reported by Time Magazine in 1938, Joseph Figlock, a local street sweeper in Detroit, Michigan, in the United States of America, was walking down the road, minding his own business, when a baby fell from a fourth storey window. The baby struck him on the head and shoulders. They were both injured, but they both survived. The following year, a two year old fell from a window, again, breaking their fall on Joseph Figlock as he was walking underneath. Again, they both survived.

Why?

"I do not believe in meaningless coincidences. I believe every coincidence is a message, a clue about a particular facet of our lives that requires our attention."   Deepak Chopra

How many times have you heard someone say 'There is no such thing as coincidence. Everything happens for a reason'. There must be a reason for coincidence, right? In which case, why do coincidences happen? What is the purpose of coincidence?

Laugh with me, dear reader, I have organized the reason for mysterious coincidences into six categories:

Guidance

Rescue/Protection

Warning

Destiny

A Reminder

For Upliftment

I have found the most common of these reasons is for Guidance. Whether it is to confirm which direction you should go, where your next steps are, who should you go to work for, or which relationship will be right for you. Questions that the Universe answers for you by offering communication in the form of coincidence.

Guidance for decision-making when you are unsure of which path to take. Guidance in literal ways, you can literally be guided by signs from the Universe not just metaphysically in relation to your life choices, but also in order to put you in the right place at the right time to receive ideas and inspiration or to meet up with your latest brilliant opportunity.

Guidance

Alice: Would you tell me, please, which way I ought to go from here?

Cat: That depends a good deal on where you want to get to

Alice: I don't much care where

Cat: Then it doesn't matter which way you go

(Alice's Adventures in Wonderland), Carroll, 1865

We can see coincidences as signposts on the journey of life. Showing us whether the path is the right or wrong direction for us depending on where we want to be, from the place where we are currently standing.

Confirmation you are on the right path. Signs to serve as confirmation to keep heading in your current direction. Lining you up to experience the coincidence for no other reason than to confirm you are on the right path.

Confirmation of a new path. Signs that have nothing to do with what you are thinking about for your material goals in life, nothing to do with what your personality wants, you have a higher aspect calling you over to 'look at this, over here...' calling you over... 'change direction, walk this way, come this way'. Guidance to let you know that there is another path.

Clarification of which path to take. When you are feeling lost/confused and you are unsure of which path to take. Help from the Universe for you to choose the best path for you. The sign itself doesn't cause you to make the decision, but how you feel in response to the sign is what you need to be looking at.

It is an old therapy tool, if you are having trouble making a choice of two paths, pretend you have made the choice of the first path. How does it feel? Then pretend you have made the choice of the second path. How does it feel? You will know from how you feel, which path you need to take. It is the same with signs and coincidence. Trusting your inner feeling will help you to make the right decision.

Confirmation you are on the wrong path. An interruption signal. Something will happen to alert you that you are heading in the wrong direction. You could be heading for a fall.

Rescue/Protection

These rescuing events can happen in various degrees of severity. Everything from protecting you from having something ruin your clothes (like your alarm not going off, making you late for work. As you are walking past a housepainter he drops a tin of paint, which would have splashed on you if you had been on time) right through to rescues which seem miraculous because they are lifesaving. With the internet at our fingertips, there are a whole host of stories out there which do the rounds on Youtube pretty much daily.

The Rescues which have strange coincidences because of the relationship between the people involved, do tend to gather the most momentum and news of these events are the most likely to go viral. What once would have meant that everyone in a town would have heard about it, has now spread to a global audience.

Rescue can also happen when people find themselves in need of less dramatic help, such as, having a car stuck in the mud, only for a farmer to drive by on a tractor, just happening to drive by and be in a position to help. Test the Universe for yourself. Put something useful in your bag and see how long it takes for someone to need it.

Something like a plaster, painkillers, some tissues, something that people often find themselves caught out by not having one.

I have found that if I carry a spare plastic bag and a packet of tissues, I tend to see people drop their shopping on the floor in front of me, and voila, I am able to produce my spare carrier bag. If I have tissues, guaranteed I will come across someone crying, or someone who has an insect in their eye, or someone in need of my rescuing tissues because they have spilt their coffee of any other myriad of reasons us little humans need tissues.

Esther Hicks tells the story of how she used to arm herself with a coat hanger in case anyone locked themselves out of their car. She would see people all the time in need of her coat hanger to break into their locked cars.

It wasn't until she let three people into their locked cars in one day that she realised she needed to stop taking the coat hanger out! Her belief in the Law of Attraction is that she was putting herself in the right place at the right time to be able to use the hanger. If she didn't have the hanger on her, she wouldn't be the person lining up with the person in need of it. If you do take to carrying a First Aid Kit about, be prepared for the consequences.

Exploding Church Story

In 1950, every single member of a church choir was running late for their weekly choir practice. Every week on Wednesday at 7.20 pm the choir met for practice. Even the Choir Director was running late. At 7.27 pm, Wednesday March 1st 1950, the church exploded due to a natural gas leak. West Side Baptist Church in Beatrice, Nebraska blew up. Not one soul was harmed because all 15 members of the choir were running late. What are the chances?

Warnings

Warnings are also given by way of coincidence. If only we are aware enough, and with enough belief, to be able to accept the warnings, understand and interpret their meaning, often the Universe helps us before we make all sorts of mistakes. How many stories have you heard about disastrous weddings which turned into disastrous marriages? Thunder and lightning on a wedding day which caused flooding and really should have halted the wedding, but the vicar and the guests all waded through 2 feet of water as if to insist the ceremony take place. People say 'I should have known, all the signs were there'.

Warnings about impending disaster, death, and even poor decisions. Once you have strengthened your commitment to accepting that there is a higher source of Self, of which you are a part, it does become easier to heed the warnings, pay attention and listen to your own guidance system.

Destiny

Synchronicities which are going to happen regardless of what is happening for us in our lives. Sometimes coincidence happens because fate is knocking on the door. Often this type of coincidence has an extreme transformational effect on the person who is having the experience.

When the coincidence has a profound effect on our lives, acting as a catalyst for change, it can feel mystical. The whole experience can leave us with a feeling that something has happened to us, rather than through us, we have been overtaken by an event, we entered a zone where our thoughts, feelings and actions just went through the motions in order to keep up with the events surrounding us.

There are some events in life which can feel pre-destined. As if this is something which was going to happen, no matter what we did. It was our Fate, our Destiny.

A little story borrowed from Greek Mythology, dear reader, ancient Greek mythology which talks of the three old crones. In Greek mythology, the Fates, also known as the Moirai, are the three goddesses who determine the destiny of individuals and gods. The Fates control the thread of life and shape the events of existence.

I have ChatGPT to thank for the next few paragraphs dear reader. I am sure ChatGPT could probably have created an easier-to-read version of this whole book, but where would be the fun in that?

In Greek mythology, the Fates, also known as the Moirai (singular: Moira), are a group of three goddesses who preside over destiny, and control the thread of life for both mortals and gods. The Fates are often depicted as weavers or spinners of fate, determining the course of human lives from birth to death. The three Moirai are:

Clotho; Lachesis and Atropos:

Clotho (the Spinner): She spins the thread of life, determining a person's birth and the events that will unfold.

Lachesis (the Allotter): She measures the thread of life, determining the length and destiny of a person's life.

Atropos (the Cutter): She cuts the thread of life, determining the moment of death and the end of a person's life.

Interesting. The power of three. Three women with different roles yet are dependent on each other. I notice there are a lot of stories around the subject of death, and I am sure there is a whole book worth of stories out there. The sort of thing that happens around the time of death, you know, clocks stopping, landlines ringing and there is no-one there, no-one speaking when you pick up the handset. Waking up in the middle of the night for no apparent reason, only to discover later than someone we care deeply about has died, at that exact time.

A phone call to wake us up, so we are already weirdly awake and in a better place to take the worst news from the next phone call, which is bringing news of a death. Sometimes people have reported a visit (by the spirit of the recently deceased person) to their bedroom before they had even heard the news of their death.

Triple Ship Sinking Survivor Story

Some people have such extreme life events that it is difficult to see how it can be anything but fate. Violet Jessop was a nurse who survived three different ship sinkings. This nurse was on the Olympic, the Titanic and the Britannic and survived all three ship sinkings.

Missing Aeroplane Story

A Dutch cyclist (Maartin de Jonge) escaped death not

once, but twice. He was meant to be on the missing Malaysia flight MH370 and he was also meant to be on the Malaysia flight MH17 that was shot down in 2014. Last minute change of plans led to his life being saved.

A reminder from our Guardian Angels

Imagine being our Guardian Angels trying to communicate with us? How much 'in your face', straight-up, bone-shaking coincidence does there have to be for you to a) acknowledge the event and b) realise the importance and intelligence behind the event?

One of my favourite motivators/self-help innovators was Wayne Dyer, and it is with some sadness that I use the past-tense. Wayne Dyer, along with Esther and Jerry Hicks have long been world leaders in helping people to help themselves. Esther and Jerry Hicks are happy to communicate with 'Infinite Intelligence' they call it. Drawing information from an unseen source to help us little humans out, in yet another hour of need.

In some of Esther Hicks workshops, which can be found on YouTube and on her website www.abraham-hicks.com people often tell stories of communication from the Other Side. Or Source. Or people who are no longer living. Or as Esther says, from people who have croaked.

As I was writing this book, I was listening to a YouTube recording of one of the Abraham workshops, usually held on a cruise ship, which does look amazing. I digress, back to the recording. There I was, in Essex, Southend-on-Sea, to be precise, with a lot on my plate, too much to worry about, so I ran a lovely hot bath and settled down to an Abraham Hicks recording to help soothe my mind.

There was a man speaking, of his synchronistic experience he had which involved Wayne Dyer. How, wonderful, I was in exactly the right place at the right time on my seemingly random Youtube offering, it was a suggestion from Youtube, not a recording I had chosen specifically. The man said he had been listening to Wayne Dyer tapes and he had loved the recordings so much that he had sent them out to a couple of friends and his sister with a request that they return the tapes re-wound.

This would save him a little time, leaving him less work to do before sending the tapes out to the next set of people he had on his list who he felt would benefit from the beautiful, soothing, relaxing sound of Wayne Dyer's voice.

This man, let's call him Dave, had sent a tape to his sister when she was alive. His sister had passed away, three years to the day that he was looking at the tapes which had been returned to him. After the death of his sister he hadn't got around to re-sending the tapes to other people, he felt the loss of his sister deeply and as he looked at the tapes he realised the one tape from his sister hadn't actually been re-wound.

Dave put the tape into the cassette player and listened to the words being spoken by Wayne Dyer, who was talking about psychic awareness, telepathy and the intuition that comes from just thinking about someone and then suddenly, out of the blue, hearing from them.

He heard Wayne speak the words:

"Just suppose you hadn't heard from your sister in three years…"

Dave's sister had died three years ago to the day. Dave was still very upset about the loss of his sister, to him, hearing those words at that time wasn't proof enough, or evidential enough, that they weren't just a coincidence. Dave sent a prayer up:

'If you are there and you can hear me, send me a message'.

The next day Dave received an unexpected letter through the mail from the Philippines from a lady he had been communicating with for years. Dave had been sending financial donations and in return the lady sent a report back to Dave explaining that she had bought trainers for her daughter, or whatever she had used his money for, she wrote and kept him posted.

This day, the letter which arrived wasn't just the usual shopping list of what had been purchased. This letter had been written in capital letters, unlike the usual words the lady in the Philippines would have sent, along the lines of 'Thank you for everything you have done' and she signed it off 'Your Eternal Sister'.

Now Dave was absolutely blown away by that coincidence, he didn't feel it was simply coincidental, he felt that the lady from the Philippines had been used as a messenger by his sister, to get a message to him. Dave was also amazed that by the time he had made the request, the letter was already in the post.

Dave was so stunned he contacted the lady in the Philippines in order to try and find out what had prompted her to write these foreign words out of the blue. Dave discovered there had been an earthquake in the Philippines, leading to the deaths of three people, his little lady being one of them. He never found out why she wrote those words.

As Esther Hicks responded, this level of synchronicity, for Source, the Universe, Infinite Intelligence, is simply Child's Play.

Upliftment

Some coincidences are for positive affirmation, something to offer you hope and happiness. Something which has special meaning for you and therefore will help you to feel uplifted by it. For no other reason than to help you to feel better.

Or maybe all the categories, reasons, and groups that I have come up with, all boil down to making you feel better. Don't all coincidences, no matter what the purpose or the reason, help to uplift us? Remind us that our life has meaning, we are loved and we are looked after and protected by an Intelligence that we can't see, but we can learn to trust and have faith in.

While I am here, join with me dear reader, in sending up a little thought of gratitude, a little appreciation for all the coincidences that have shown up so far. For helping us little humans to keep going on the difficult paths that are our life journeys. No-one on the planet has an easy life. No-one.

Here are some signs that your Guardian Angels are prompting you and uplifting your spirit:

You feel a new burst of energy, you have a happy excited feeling of boosted thoughts.

You feel connected to a stream of feeling happy, passionate energy, ideas, love, warmth, feelings of safety and connectedness, certainty.

You are feeling good, you are in exactly the right place at the right time to download life-changing ideas.

You feel the urge to de-clutter your emotional baggage, your negative thinking, and even the actual clutter in your home.

You are coming up with life-altering ideas. Resources are coming in the form of really good ideas, pertinent, applicable to you, relevant to your life and the next big step or little step, moving forward, feeling like growth or progress.

You resonate strongly with the information. It feels exactly right for you to believe. Other people might not believe you; they may think it weird, but it doesn't feel weird to you.

You are prompted to binge watch something, extreme information gathering about your subject, you cannot get enough of the subject which has piqued your interest, you are thirsty for the books, the films, the audio, the YouTube videos. You cannot get enough of your subject.

You continue on the path of that information stream. You feel as though you are having downloads from psychic thoughts, or even spaces in the material world, in the form of information from YouTube, the library, or even the bookshop.

How?

Our attention is drawn to the coincidence. The information is brought to us either directly or indirectly. How this can happen is through our mind, psychically, we can also see it with our own eyes, we can hear it through our ears, we can feel our way intuitively towards a coincidence, we can find ourselves drawn to the coincidence. The Infinite

Intelligence of the Universe is gently guiding and putting us in place to experience the phenomenon that is synchronicity.

Synchronicity is the Universe returning your Game. The Universe playing back with you. The Universe is returning your call.

Pay attention. Be mindful. Acknowledge the event. Thank the Universe for the coincidence. Literally say Thank You. Either doff your cap, or touch your collar or give a little wave, or whatever physical action you can come up with that you feel comfortable with, make that a habit as a way to respond to a coincidence showing up in your world. You know when some people see a magpie, they hold their collar until they see an animal? Or they say 'Morning Mr Magpie...' these little actions which, although they do have their origins in superstition, encourage the Universe to dish you up some more. The more you notice coincidence, the more you find a little bit of time in your day to put yourself on the wavelength of appreciation and paying attention causes more coincidences to show up.

When a coincidence comes your way, the most appropriate response is gratitude. Gratitude of having had a coincidence happen in your life experience and gratitude for the fact that you have spotted it.

Even more gratitude if the event has a deep meaning

for you and you are able to feel a sense of awe, inspired by the higher intelligence that has orchestrated synchronicity and lined it up in perfect symmetry, just for you. It is a little 'Hello' from God, the Universe, your Higher Self, however you refer to the energy field that creates worlds that surrounds us every day, that we are living through.

The coincidences can show up in the form of

written words

spoken words

sung words/song lyrics

numbers

suburban messages

signs on the side of vans or lorries

marketing slogans

common phrases

symbols

pictures on signs

images

feelings

hunches

We are magnets in the Universe. We are attracting to us whatever and whoever we are thinking about. We attract more of how we feel. Things, people and thoughts which vibrate on our level, will be drawn to us and we will be drawn their way.

How do you respond to the Universe playing with you? Do you laugh? Enjoying the experience? The Universe will dish you up more things to laugh at. Keep smiling and find more things to laugh about!

The other side of this coin is that if you are miserable, unhappy, and ungrateful, with your eyes closed to the wonder of everyday miracles around you, the Universe still respects your free will, and you have the freedom to ignore the Universe's best efforts to get your attention. The Universe will keep showing you things for you to ignore. The ignoring bit is your choice, it is your free will, your power, your choice. The Universe is still there, day in, day out, churning out miraculous events.

Learning to enjoy coincidences is one step toward enjoying life. If anyone in your world has lost faith or hope or is feeling down with no sign of perking up, (often after having had some unwanted life experience), and you want to help pick them back up, you could start with coincidence. All it takes is one small coincidence to change a person's emotional state and quite possibly their life path.

Increasing Synchronicities

Everyone enjoys feeling good. People flock to people when they are happy, feeling good, laughing, smiling, feeling expansive, generous and pleasant to be around.
The opposite is also true, misery loves company. Maybe the company of other miserable people.

It is important for you to enjoy your life; part of that process is to learn to enjoy what you have. If you haven't learnt the importance of feeling good, start with coincidence. Once you begin to find pleasure in coincidences, they will increase, bringing you more pleasure, this is how the Universe works.

To appreciate coincidence, you have to match up with the vibrational level. For 'vibrational level', read 'emotional state'.

The Abraham-hicks emotional scale shows an obvious range of feelings. Whatever you believe about the law of attraction, this emotional guidance scale is a great example of states of feelings:

Powerlessness

Insecurity

Guilt

Jealousy

Hatred

Rage

Anger

Worry

Doubt

Impatience

Irritation

Frustration

Pessimism

This is the lower half of the scale, and right in the middle, from where your emotional state could go either way: Boredom.

Although this is the balancing part of this scale, I feel this is also the danger zone. This is often the point where people reach for artificial stimulants to relieve this state, rather than finding better feeling thoughts which will lead to the more positive half of the scale:

Positive Expectation

Contentment

Belief

Hopefulness

Optimism

Enthusiasm

Happiness

Passion

Eagerness

Love

Empowered

Joy

Freedom

Of course, you can notice the coincidences whilst feeling any of these emotional states. Any feelings on the bottom half of the scale, anything lower than boredom, are often as a response to very real, sad situations or life events, sometimes the emotions are too overwhelming for people to notice the coincidences, or the meaningful element of coincidence takes a backseat to the emotional pain currently being felt by the person.

The higher up the emotional scale you are feeling, the easier it is to be able to appreciate synchronicity. Feeling awe, wonder and delight, is a beautiful feeling response to meaningful coincidence.

The Universe also shows you to yourself, acting as a mirror, so if crappy things are showing up, you do need to look at your negative beliefs, your judgments against other people, things, events and life generally.

This is how you can measure what sort of vibrations you are giving off. How are the people you are surrounded by behaving? Are they happy? Or are they complaining? Are they suffering? Are they grateful? Whereabouts are you living in this benevolent universe? As Einstein said, there is only one question you need to ask yourself in life: 'Is the Universe a friendly or a hostile place?'

I do believe we all travel along the journey of self-discovery which brings us different levels of understanding and belief. There are times when we need to rest in order to grow and there are times when we need to take action in order to grow.

Life is such a mystery and it is the mystery, the not knowing, which makes it interesting. As Wayne Dyer said, 'No-one knows enough to be a pessimist'. It doesn't stop people being pessimistic, but just that idea that you never know for sure, what could be around the corner, should be enough to bring a feeling of hope. Another mantra of mine

'You never know who you are going to meet'.

Carl Jung wrote about a link between emotional intensity and synchronicity quoted by Begg in his book; Synchronicity; (Begg, 2001). In Carl Jung's book, *Synchronicity* (1955) Jung quotes from a text by St. Albertus Magnus. Thanks to Begg for quoting Jung in his book, and now I too am repeating the same quote, from Jung's *'Synchronicity, An Acausal Connecting Principle'* Carl Jung felt the key to synchronicity was an emotional intensity:

"I discovered an instructive account [of magic] in Avicenna's Libera sextus naturalium, which says that a certain power to alter things indwells in the human soul and subordinates the other things to her, particularly when she is swept into a great excess of love or hate or the like. When therefore the soul of a man falls into a great excess of any passion, it can be proved by experiment that it (the excess) binds things (magically) and alters them in the way it wants, and for a long time I did not believe it, but after I had read the necromantic books and other of the kind on signs and magic, I found that the emotionality of the human soul is the chief cause of all these things, whether because, on account of her great emotion, she alters her bodily substance and the other things towards which she strives, or because, on account of her dignity, the other, lower things are subject to her, or because of the appropriate hour or astrological situation or another power coincides with so inordinate an emotion, and we (in consequence) believe that what this power does is then done by the soul...

Whoever would learn the secret of doing or undoing these things must know that everyone can influence everything magically if he falls into a great excess...and he must do it at that hour when the excess befalls him

,and operate with the things which the soul prescribes.

For the soul is then so desirous of the matter she would accomplish that of her own accord she seizes the more significant and better astrological hour which also rules over the things suited to that matter...Thus it is the soul who desires a thing more intensely, who makes things more effective and more like what comes forth...Such is the manner of production with everything the soul intensely desires. Everything she does with that aim in view possesses motive power and efficacy for what the soul desires."

J.G. Bennett The Dramatic Universe, Vol. II Hodder & Stoughton, 1961 'Harxis'.

Notice what the Universe is bringing to you. Acknowledge what you have chosen to notice and pay attention to. What has drawn your attention, out of all the information which you are surrounded by, what has caught your eye?

Acknowledge which parts you have given extra attention to, by either talking about it to someone or writing it down.

Keep a diary of your synchronicities and coincidences. Particularly the ones you want to see more of.

I have left some pages at the back of this book for you to use to record your own personal coincidence stories throughout the year. A page for each month, you can use the pages for more than one year.

Lining up with the Universe

You don't have to do anything to line up with the Universe. You are already in it. There are things you can do to level up. If you see the Universe as a game we are playing, albeit a game which may feel like it never lets up, there are definite improved human states we can experience which does change whatever the Universe is delivering to the inbox of our life.

It is impossible not to be in tune with the Universe. But are you vibrating with the out-of-tune, something discordant, or are you in harmony?

Try lining yourself up with an expectation of benefiting from a benevolent Universe and see what transpires. Working hard, doing the preparation and staying aligned with who you really are. Otherwise known as being Lucky.

Some people are blessed with luck. The Luck of the Irish, you know, those blarney stone kissing lucky people. Some people are blessed with disaster! Either way, we are all blessed. Finding yourself in the right place at the right time to find the right job, the right relationship, the right housing, the right car, does mean you are in a healthy place. Physically, mentally, emotionally, spiritually, you are in tune with the Universe.

Giving up feeling pessimistic, letting go of cynicism, treating the Universe as if it is a friendly place which is just there to serve you, to deliver whatever you are asking for. The Universe reflects back to you exactly whatever you are giving out, so if you are giving out a willingness to serve, the Universe will serve back.

Knitted Hat Story

I play a game every winter, with the Universe. I find something that a homeless person needs, or I make something and then I go out on the streets at night and find a person who could use it, like a sleeping bag or a portable pillow, or gloves or a hat, something small and easy to carry.

One year I downloaded a knitting pattern, a fabulous knitted hat pattern which was really easy to make. Since I am a natty knitter, I re-created the pattern, added some stars and used glittery, sparkly wool. It was fun. It was my little project to play with the Universe.

Once I had knitted the hats, I made four of them altogether, different colours and patterns. I was planning on taking them out, allowing the Universe to guide me to the people who could use a natty knitted hat.

The day I finished them, it was a Saturday before Christmas, it started snowing, it was bitterly cold and I didn't even want to head out to do my good deeds, but I had been knitting all week and I had promised myself, and the Universe. I knew that the Universe will have lined up co-operative components, ie, other people, in need of my hats. I couldn't let them down. I wrapped up warm, wearing my thickest coat, my own warm hat, scarf, gloves, boots, you name it, I was wearing it.

I walked through Southend Town Centre and across town to the roughest part of the town where I saw a man walking towards me, clutching the hand of a little girl, neither of them looked particularly well fed, or warm, and neither of them had hats. I waved my carrier bag in his direction, and caught his eye, which was screwed up against the icy snow blowing in his face.

'Do you need a hat?' I asked.

He looked at me suspiciously. His little girl looked expectantly at me. I rummaged in my carrier bag and pulled out a sparkly pink number, handing it over to the little girl's dad, she was clinging to him, uncertain about taking anything from strangers.

He laughed and said 'Thank you'.

He gave her the hat and they walked away. I watched her wrestle her new pink hat onto her jet black hair as the snow continued to play with all of us. My face was stinging from the cold and I had only been out for twenty minutes, I had had enough.

As willing as I was, I didn't fancy getting pneumonia,

so I cheated. I walked to the office of the Samaritans and hung the carrier bag on the door. The Universe understood, it blew me all the way back home into the warm where I recovered and enjoyed the memory of the little girl's face as she realised the pink sparkly hat with cat ears was coming her way.

Chapter II
Categories of Coincidence

1) Psychic Phenomenon
2) Life Events
3) Nature
4) Animals
5) People
6) Physical experience
7) Inanimate Objects
8) Spiritual
9) Information (data stream)
10) Numbers

The Universe has written you a love letter in the form of your whole life. The Universe kisses us with coincidence. Coincidences are the loving nudges and gifts which can keep us going on our life path. Considering the size of the Universe and our role in it, it would be easy to think ourselves forgotten. Left in the flotsam and jetsam of uncontrolled atoms, to be buffered about by the Universe over which we seemingly have little or no control. Coincidence can act as a reminder that we are being held by a higher intelligence.

Our life journey is not going without notice. We are not unobserved. We are loved, we are looked after, there is a purpose for each of our lives, and one way for us to be reminded that there is a benevolent, higher power, an infinite intelligence, at work, on our behalf is to have a coincidence show up for us.

I think all coincidences are pretty unexplainable, really. Therefore, all synchronicity belongs in the category of 'Unexplained'. Some coincidences have an air of mystery which is beyond explanation on any level. I have attempted to compartmentalise the information to try and make some sense out of the synchronicities.

After scratching my head for a while, I juggled the information, threw it into the air and let it group itself as naturally as it could. Ten categories emerged and formed groups of types of coincidence.

I have tried to tidy the data into ten clouds of stuff, which sometimes overlap or intertwine. I use the term 'clouds' intentionally, the groups are fluffy with no clear boundaries. My apologies if I have put some examples in a category that you wouldn't have done. Some of the information straddles more than one category.

Category 1
Psychic Phenomenon

"We often dream about people with whom we receive a letter by the next post. I have ascertained on several occasions that at the moment when the dream occurred, the letter was already lying in the Post Office of the addressee."

C.G.Jung, Synchronicity (1955)

Synchronicities come to us through many sources. In this category I am focusing on the channel of our minds, through our thoughts, either while we are awake, asleep, or in meditation. All sorts of weird experiences happen through our little minds, telepathy, precognition, premonition and even shared dreams. I think déjà vu probably falls into this category.

Carl Jung invented the term 'Synchronicity'. One of the most famous coincidence stories in the world, I am sure, was the moment when Carl Jung was mid-therapy session with a client who had been talking about a dream involving a golden scarab beetle.

As he was listening to his client explain her dream, he heard a tapping on the window. Not only did he pay attention to the distraction, but he opened the window and grabbed the source of the tapping, it was a golden scarab beetle.

The very same insect that his client was talking about, right at that exact moment. He had the presence of mind to catch the insect and hand it to his client. This beautiful sequence of synchronistic events led his client to have a profound sense of psychological shift because it held such deep meaning for her. (Psychology Today, 2023)

Dreams

Talking about psychic events and dreams can be quite difficult. Not just because of any reticence to express the experience, for fear of being thought crazy or unhinged, but because it can be so hard to explain to another person, the meaning that it has for us, personally. A bit like attempting to explain the meaning of a dream.

Only the person who has the dream can really uncover the meaning of their dreams. Other people can hazard a guess, but explain your dreams at your peril. It is easy for other people to be so certain about the meaning of your dream that they can trample all over the subtleties of the energies that brought you the information in your sleep.

For instance, you might dream of moving house. You mention your dream to your neighbour. She takes this as the opportunity to mention a friend of hers who is looking to move into the neighbourhood. Before you know it you have a buyer for your house, and you are looking to literally move. That could actually become a Thing that happens in your life, and it all began with a dream.

Or, the dream could have been your subconscious knocking on the doorway to your waking state to let you know that something needs looking at. You know, something going on for you emotionally, that needs attention, somewhere, something or someone you need to move on from, some feeling that has become stuck and needs clearing out and moving away from. An emotional state that you have been holding yourself in.

I do feel very strongly that your dreams are a form of communication that is meant just for your interpretation, just for your own personal understanding. Before you share your dreams, make sure you have your boundaries in place so that you are not influenced by anyone else misunderstanding or misinterpreting them for you. I think it could be the same with synchronicity. Stick to your first interpretation of what it means for you.

Child's White Sock Story

Another personal coincidence story for you, dear lovely reader. I am trying to do these stories justice, but they are so personal to me, that I realise that not everyone is going to be able to resonate with my words, and that is okay. I would ask you to try it for yourself. Stay in touch with your inner being. Play with your subconscious in your sleep and see what shows up!

I do believe that having a dream diary, or a dream journal, a little book specially designated for the purpose of keeping a record of your dreams, upon waking, sends a message to your subconscious that you are paying attention and therefore increases the number of dreams that you experience.

Also, there is the practicality of helping you to remember your dreams by writing them down as soon as you wake up. Dreams are soon forgotten once you start processing your waking reality and easily let go of by your waking mind.

This story comes from a time in my life where there was a regular amount of stress, not a vast amount of stress, just a manageable, regular amount. I was a single parent of a teenage boy. I had a lovely, busy, challenging life. Part of that life involved studying for a degree and working part-time jobs which allowed room for my studies.

One of those jobs was selling things on eBay, this was

before Amazon blew up. I used to absolutely love receiving a notification on my email letting me know when I had sold something. You know that punch the air feeling! A cause for celebration! Money coming in. I loved it. Making money without leaving the house. I sold books, clothes, toys, DVDs, make-up, and anything I felt people would buy.

I didn't have access to any computer programmes which could tell me what the best things would be to sell, to who or for how much. I had no access to data analysis to help me optimize profits or any other data comparisons which, frankly, if I had access to, I probably wouldn't have known what to do with them anyway. I was guessing, and it was hit and miss, profit wise. I enjoyed it, and it didn't feel like work. I was happy to do it after my day job, often working until midnight, during weekends and holidays, it was fun, it kept me busy and it made some money that I needed at the time.

One day, one of my oldest friends came to visit and she mentioned that she had cleared her loft out and she had loads of stuff for the charity shop. Naturally, I offered to sell it for her on eBay. As an expert level seller, I knew that I could sell her stuff in half the time it would take her to figure out how to even list one or two items. As with everything else, the more you do something, the more efficient you become at it.

My friend brought round some bags of clothes for me to sell. I put the bags in my living room. That night I went to sleep thinking I would get up early on Sunday morning and list all of her stuff. That night I had one of those dreams that I wasn't sure was a dream. Have you ever had one of those experiences where you feel as if you are awake and actually 'there', having a real conversation with a person in your dream? This is what happened to me.

I dreamt that I was in a house, in a room with a table and a man was sitting at the table in a very relaxed, casual manner. I do believe now that this man was/is my spirit guide. I had no idea who he was at the time. I felt as though I knew him, but I really didn't know him. It felt like I was meeting an old friend. He had a soft smile as though he had been here before and I was old hat. I felt almost indignant, like, 'What?!' with an attitude as though I knew everything, what did he want from me?

I felt like a teenager being held to account by someone who clearly did know better than me and I had a feeling as if I didn't want to be told. I felt as though I had been called in front of an employer when I hadn't done anything wrong. A weird feeling that is difficult to describe, because he didn't feel like a tough boss or an authority figure that I wouldn't have felt as if I didn't have a right to say 'What?' to, but he did have a sense of 'knowing' more than I did. Not in terms of information but in terms of a bigger picture, I felt he had more of a picture than I had. I don't know how I knew that.

I knew that we had a relationship, I knew that I knew him, but my logical mind knew that I had no idea who he was. He gestured towards the door. An open doorway, that didn't actually have a door in the door frame. I looked through the doorway and I could see things flying about in a room on the other side of the doorway. I walked towards the doorway, almost as if I was directed by this Being. I sort of 'knew' that I had to walk into the room, which I did. The room was full of butterflies, just flying around me.

They flew all around the room and I stood in the middle of the room, non-plussed, mystified, having no idea what I was doing there. There was another exit doorway from the room. I knew that I had to walk through the next doorway into another room.

In this room there were also loads of little things flying about and at first I couldn't tell what they were, until one flew past my face, It was a little white sock, a child's sock, a whole room full of little white socks, flying about, just like the butterflies in the first room.

It didn't even make sense at the time. You know how sometimes in a dream you can find yourself doing random things, like, towing a giraffe behind your elephant that is riding roller-skates, and it doesn't seem out of place or weird at the time, well this wasn't that. This was a feeling of being aware that something out of the ordinary was happening, but I had no explanation for it.

The next day I woke up feeling as if I had a strange experience in my sleep. I started work straightaway, firing up the computer and logging in to eBay, prepping my friend's clothes ready for sale. This involved using a clothes hanger to hang the clothes up on a dado rail in order to take photos. I hung up a shirt, took some pictures, removed the shirt and hung the hanger back on the dado rail while I put the shirt in the 'done' pile and sorted through for the next item to photograph.

As I turned away from the hanger, it fell off the dado rail and dropped behind a radiator. I couldn't fit my hand behind the radiator to grab the hanger. I used another hanger to reach down and pull the first hanger out. As I pulled, I heard a 'clink' as I jagged on something plastic behind the radiator.

As I pulled the hanger out I noticed it had something attached to it, a piece of white material. I pulled on the material and freed it from the hanger. It was a little white sock, a child-size sock. I took the hanger and felt behind the radiator again, having a rummage with the hanger to see what had made the clunking noise. A cube dropped out the bottom of the radiator. A plastic cube, a child's toy. I picked it up and looked at it. It had a picture moulded into the plastic; it was a picture of a butterfly.

I had a surreal moment, knowing that my dream had been 'broken'. As the phrase goes, you know when someone says something that reminds you of a dream you had, you say 'You broke my dream'. The dream from the previous night came flooding back to me. The butterflies and the little white socks. I was literally standing in my living room, holding a child-size white sock and looking at a butterfly picture on the side of a child's toy cube.

I couldn't believe it. What was that? I had no idea the sock was behind the radiator. It wasn't my son's sock. We had only moved into that flat when my son was around 12. We didn't have any young children's toys or child-size socks. It did feel as though I was having a strange, unexplained surreal experience.

As strange as that felt, it wasn't the end of the story, dear reader. A few months later I was browsing on eBay through the psychic readings, tarot cards, all things weird and wonderful and I came across a person who was offering psychic art for a small fee.

The idea being that an artist links psychically with your spirit guide, draws them and sends you the picture. For the amount of money I was paying I wasn't expecting too much. Which of course, is not the right attitude, but I was still thinking along the lines of 'You get what you pay for'. However, I was interested enough to bid on the item and I was pleased when I heard that I had 'won' it, as the marketing on eBay does like to remind you.

You aren't just buying products, you are 'winning' at auction. Go You! It is all part of the appeal, and I was feeling the appeal of having someone send me some art of who only knows what. When the picture arrived, all wrapped nicely in a special circular art transportation, I was surprised at the amount of effort that had clearly been put into making sure the picture arrived in one piece.

When I opened the parcel I could see the image of the man in my dream looking back at me. The wry smile, the floppy brown curly hair. It was the most bizarre feeling. Apart from anything else, I was not expecting my spirit guide to look like a humble, barely conspicuous curly-haired young man. I had ideas of spirit guides looking like Gandalf from The Lord of the Rings. It was the image of the guy I had seen in my dream. If not an exact image, a pretty good likeness.

Flatmate Travelling Out of Body Experience

Another personal story, dear reader, a little experience which I am having trouble finding a category for, so I will share it and let you decide where it belongs. Travel back with me to 1988, to my experience of sharing a house with a couple of flat mates in Shoeburyness. I shared a house with a woman I had been at school with, I will call her Lisa, since I haven't asked her permission to either share the story or use her name! Lisa and I rented a house, a ridiculously cheap house. It was a three bedroomed house, for the price of a two bedroom.

The reason for that was mainly because the third bedroom was off the second bedroom. Like an ensuite to the Master, but with no bathroom in it. Whoever was in room 3, had to walk through room 2 to get down the stairs and room 2 had to put up with room 3 people walking through their bedroom. But we were young, on the main, we just didn't care. We all agreed to take turns in the shared accommodation bit, and every three months we would all change bedrooms. It was fun. We were carefree and fun-loving, no-one cared.

One Sunday morning I was lying in bed with my boyfriend in room 2. Lisa came out of room 3 wearing a black polo-neck jumper and her knickers. She walked out of her room and sat on the edge of my bed. I looked at her, she looked at me. Neither of us spoke. I thought it must be because my boyfriend was asleep and she didn't want to wake him up. Lisa got up off my bed and walked out of the bedroom and walked down the stairs. As I was lying there, I was thinking it was a bit strange that she hadn't spoken. I woke my boyfriend up and told him, as you do, that Lisa had done something strange. It really wasn't like her not to speak. The door to bedroom 3 opened again.

Lisa walked out of the bedroom wearing a black polo-neck jumper and knickers. I said to her 'What are you doing?' 'Did you just come back upstairs?' My brain couldn't compute how she was coming out of the room again. I thought maybe she had walked past me and I hadn't noticed. But no, she had no idea what I was talking about. She hadn't come out of the room the first time. I have no explanation for what happened.

Intuition

I am pretty sure that I have enough words in me about the subject of intuition to write another book about it. Intuition is really significant when knowing how to interpret signs, symbols, life events, but this book is not the place to delve into the subject any further than to recognize it's role in coincidence.

Intuition, what is it? It is that inner knowing, without the need for words, about something or someone in your world. We all have it, and some of us listen to it more than others. Intuition is the feeling of knowing when something is right for us, or when something is off. We don't always have a reason for our belief, or knowing, but learning to trust your intuition is a really useful life skill that can keep you out of all sorts of trouble.

If your intuition is telling you 'don't do it' or 'not with this person', 'not this job', 'not this home', listen to it. Your own inner voice will guide you onto the best path for you, if only you will listen.

Telepathy

Thinking of someone who several minutes later contacts you by phone, messages, Facebook, twitter, Instagram, WhatsApp, Snapchat, you name it, is a form of telepathy.

The thought of someone, passing through your mind, moments before they contact you, is a form of telepathy. As humans we can heighten our own sensory perception, some people are more intuitive than others and some people develop their skill of heightened mental awareness more than others, but I think it is a skill everyone has access to.

Some people see these skills as psychic ability, they are able to draw on a level of mental consciousness at will, for the majority of people, it happens naturally, some people even ignore it or dismiss it, but for lovers of coincidence, it is one of those areas where we can improve our own mental acuity to not only be able to recognise when it is happening, but perhaps even to voice it out loud or even call the other person who is thinking of us first.

Someone can think of us, intending to contact us, and we call them only for them to say: 'I was just thinking of you', which we often dismiss, but in reality, we are picking up on their intention to call us.

Premonition

Some feelings and thoughts bring us an awareness that some specific event will happen. Often this occurs around births, deaths, meeting significant others, and all manner of other huge life events. Sometimes this happens for us, but more often on behalf of other people.

Premonition sometimes happens just before an event occurs, split seconds, minutes, hours, days. People have been known to have the same premonitions about people.

A common premonition is around the subject of births and deaths, trauma to a family member which is similar to telepathy, feeling linked up to the other person, so when a major life event is due to happen to them, other family members are filled with feelings of unease, or sometimes a definite knowing that something has happened. It is the unexplainable, it isn't easy to explain premonition, once you have experienced it once, it does become easier to recognise.

Mark Twain Predicting his Own Death

The Author of The Adventures of Huckleberry Finn was born in 1835 on the same day as Halley's Comet appeared. In 1909 Mark Twain predicted his own time of death *'it is coming again next year*

and I expect to go out with it'.

Mark Twain did indeed, die of a heart attack, a day after Halley's Comet nearest approach to Earth, in 1910.

One of the most interesting parts of life, for me, dear reader, are the parts that we have no definite explanation for, the mysterious, the unknown and quite possibly unknowable. It often isn't easy to recount the story, never mind explaining it. This is the feeling that I am trying to convey.

Premonition in the Cinema Story

Let me set the scene a little for my next story. Come back with me to 1989, roughly. It might have been late 1988, but it was roughly around that time. A time with no internet, no google, no uber, the list of things that we have now that we didn't have then goes on and on. I mention these things as a reminder that the very act of more than a few people getting together in the same place at the same time took a lot more organisation than it does today. No Whatsapp group.

I know, for you dear younger readers it might be a stretch to even try and picture what that looked like. Well, it looked like either using the landline between houses or popping round to check what the arrangements were for the weekend. 1989 was a time of mixed fashions, big hair and aerobics for some and scootering, mods, punks, rave fashions for others. Before Facebook, if you wanted everyone to know everything about your life, you had to track them down and tell them.

I was living in a shared house with a couple of friends that I had known at school. We had a busy house. One of my flatmates was a hairdresser and often there was a kitchen full of people waiting to have their hair done. It was during these social gatherings that the plans were made for the weekend. Our other flat mate had heard that there was going to be an all-night filmfest at the local cinema, all night showings of horror movies. As a group of energy-filled young people, whenever something was going on in Southend-on-Sea, we were all over it. Desperate for entertainment and a need to socialize with people, a need which has now been satisfied with social media sharing and photo sharing sites, but that is another story!

When you think about it, it was a miracle that we managed to organise ourselves to meet up in places at the same time, and yet we all did, regularly, we would find ourselves in the same pub waiting to go to the same party or club and we did have a great time.

This is the benefit of being part of a group, there is safety in numbers and there is always someone to go out with. This particular night, after spending time together indoors at home, we all headed out to the cinema. I think there were about eight of us in our outing to the all-night horrorfest at the cinema. The plan was to watch horror films. All night. Scaring ourselves half to death and escaping from the reality of our 9 to 5, weekday lives. A chance to feel as though we had done something with our weekend. Now, I really dislike horror films, I disliked them then and I dislike them now. I avoid them if I can. I don't mind a little bit of fear, a mystery, a psychological thriller, but I really can't hack full-on horror films. I am not a fan. I am not entirely sure why I agreed to go at all.

I do remember that my flatmates wanted to go, one of them was having a goth phase, she rarely came out during daylight hours at the best of times and the idea that there was a social event happening all night, really appealed to her. I think she started it by saying she wanted to go and gradually we all joined in and caught her desire and enthusiasm.

Before we knew it, we were piling into a surprisingly busy cinema. I think we made it through one film and we were halfway through the second film when I was gripped by what I can only describe as a mixture of terror combined with what felt like an invisible force, propelling me to act.

This fear had nothing to do with what was happening on the screen. I reached for my flatmate who was sitting next to me, still glued to the giant screen in front of her. I grabbed her arm and said, 'Come on, we have to go, now'. She could see that I was deadly serious, and I wasn't messing about. I had a sense of urgency that I hadn't felt before or since. I jumped out into the aisle and without asking any questions, she followed right behind me. I raced up the stairs in the dark and burst out through a pair of double doors into the cinema lobby, I kept going, right through the Exit doors leading to the street. I held the door open for my flatmate, Lisa, who by this time was full of questions.

'What's going on?' 'What are you doing?' 'Why are we out here?'

I didn't have any answers. I replied with things like 'I don't know' 'I just had to get out'. The door flew open behind her and more people started coming out, some of them coughing and apparently crying, with red eyes.

Seconds after we left the cinema, someone had let off a tear gas canister or some sort of noxious substance that was causing people irritation and trouble breathing. The whole theatre had to be evacuated. All our friends eventually came out, also with smarting red eyes and coughing. They couldn't believe that we had got out first.

What happened? I have no idea. I just know that by acting on impulse/hunch/invisible force, I saved us both from an unpleasant experience and left us both a little gob smacked as to what had just happened. Years later I now think that maybe I picked up the evil intentions of someone else coming from the other side of the cinema and I was sensitive enough to it that I felt a strong reaction to avoid it. That is the closest I can get to a logical explanation. Of course, an illogical explanation is that something else, something unseen, was guiding me about and influencing my actions.

Precognitive consciousness

Another difficult one to explain, so I am handing this one over to ChatGPT:

'Precognitive consciousness' refers to the ability or phenomenon of perceiving or having knowledge of future events or information before they occur. It implies a form of awareness or understanding that transcends normal temporal boundaries, allowing individuals to access information about future events that has not yet happened in their current timeline.

The concept of precognitive consciousness is often associated with psychic abilities or extrasensory perception (ESP). It suggests that certain individuals may possess the capacity to tap into a higher level of awareness or intuition that enables them to gain insights into future occurrences. Another way of seeing precognitive consciousness is really when a person has a sense of 'knowing'. For them, the reality hasn't formed yet, it isn't quite concrete, and yet they know this event will occur.

Dean Radin is one person who somehow managed to

organise some mass consciousness experiments. Some experiments appear to show a change in people's awareness of huge events happening up to two hours before the event. (For further reading see: Gotpsi.org Online games).

Wreck of the Titan Story

The sinking of the Titanic (whose name means unsinkable) had some coincidences with a book written by Robert Morgan in 1898 called 'The Wreck of the Titan' (also meaning unsinkable). Morgan Robertson wrote a story about a giant ship, a fictional ocean liner.

A massive, and supposedly unsinkable ship which hit an iceberg on the starboard side, going at the same speed, with the same number of passengers as the real sinking of the Titanic in 1912.

Terence McKenna Oyster Story

Terence McKenna tells a story of how he was in Israel, in a complete state, smoking some sort drug, like marijuana. He was just thinking to himself wouldn't it be nice to have some Oysters Rockefeller, or some Belgian Chocolates and Russian Caviar, in the distance, he saw a guy walking towards him, and he sensed he had food, he had a rucksack on his back.

The guy came into his tent and sat down with him, proceeding to empty his rucksack, full of food, not just any food. He had Oysters Rockefeller, Belgian Chocolates and Russian Caviar. He had been working at a four-star hotel as a dishwasher and he had quit the job in disgust, but not before raiding the fridge and filling his backpack full of food. The coincidence was so delicious for McKenna that he didn't even bother to tell the guy that he had picked up this information from the Universe just before the reality of the information reached him.

Terence McKenna, by offering the flow of spirituality, feeling loving, feeling kind, offering harmonious vibes, feelings, thoughts and words put him n the right frame of being to be able to commune with the Universe about something in his vibrational vicinity, perhaps making him aware of what was about to come to him, and McKenna took this to be something he was thinking.

Cat Predicting Deaths Story

Animals have been known to have a precognitive awareness in their waking hours, often being aware that a person is near death, or when they are about to have a fit or a heart attack, or even if they are suffering from cancer (by identifying a smell peculiar to the urine of cancer sufferers).

There was a nursing home which had a cat who would predict the next person who would be dying, by sleeping on their bed.

After the cat slept on their bed, in the next day or so, the person would usually have passed on. It happened often enough for the story to make a local tv news programme. (For further reading see: Oscar therapy cat).

Category 2
Life Events

"Well, look who I ran into" crowed Coincidence.

"Please" flirted Fate, this was meant to be.

"Pipe the heck down or get a room" growled Pessimism.

(Joseph Gordon-Levitt)

Recurring interactions, such as people giving way in their cars. Being asked for directions. Being asked for a light. Being asked for change. Being asked to take a parcel in for a neighbour. Being asked for help in any way. Being asked for a lift. Being offered a lift. These interactions are not irrelevant in the Spiritual Realm. Every interaction matters and how you handle it is everything.

Do you know the Way?

Being asked for directions. To places which have meaning.

There are a few stages of this process:

Stage One: Being asked for directions to places you don't know, and you can't help, but people ask you anyway. You think nothing of it.

Stage Two: Being asked for directions to places you feel you should know. Afterwards you find out where the place was, so you learn something. You are reminded that you don't know everything and there is always something new to learn.

Stage Three: Being asked for directions by people who happen to be on the same path as you, you are just on their path, you are the person they need. You know the way; you are able to show them the way.

Stage Four: Being asked for directions by people who stop their journeys to speak to you, they pull over in their cars (despite this age of google and satnavs) to ask for your help. You do know the way, and you are able to help.

Stage Five: Being asked for directions to a place which has deep meaning for you. You don't make the connection at the time; you just help the person in need of directions.

Stage Six: Being asked for a direction to a place which has a deep meaning for you, a place where you have a significant memory of, or a coincidental name and you have the presence of mind to share that information with the person asking.

Stage Seven: Being asked for directions to somewhere which has meaning or coincidence for you by a person who is on the same level of awareness that there is synchronicity happening, right now, in this moment of meeting, and you are able to have a chat with this person to uncover where the synchronicity is.

This is a great game to play with the Universe, a way to test your own presence and sense of self-awareness. When I first noticed that I was always asked for Directions, this is how the process unfolded for me. Sometimes I am so wrapped up in my own thoughts, my own day-to-day business that I forget the significance of the meeting and as I walk away, I think 'I have done it again, I have missed the opportunity to uncover the coincidence'. Never mind, there will always be another time.

I also like to play with the Universe by noticing birds, and flying objects, things that can easily be guided by the wind onto my path, this, of course, includes balloons. I do love to see an unexpected balloon, for me this has come in the form of blue balloons, usually, but not always. I think this began after reading Pam Grout's book about flirting with the Universe, E3, P.Grout (2014).

Pam asks her readers to test the Universe, you know, try it, why not? See how many blue balloons you can conjure up. So, I put the idea out to the Universe that I was going to manifest a blue balloon, sure enough, that happened, frequently.

I took photos, I posted to Facebook, I documented my little experience with friends and family. Some of them thought I had lost my mind, some of them humoured me, but I persisted. I know that we are all in the middle of life experiences where we feel we are on our own, but really, we are not alone, the Universe has our back. There are huge unseen forces we have at our disposal if only we can learn to tap into them.

Being Asked for Directions in Westcliff Story

So, back to my story of being asked for directions, I am not digressing completely over the blue balloon, it is part of the back story. There I was, walking along, admittedly with my headphones on, which does shut out the reality of noises and the real world. I am guilty of escaping into my own music-induced world. It makes the walk home quicker; and I had a couple of miles to go, carrying heavy shopping bags. I noticed a woman walking towards me, carrying a blue balloon, a Happy Birthday 'You Are One', balloon. I wasn't in the mood for a coincidence, frankly, I wanted to carry my shopping home, I was halfway home and moving heavy bags a couple of miles is a bit like a gym workout and I was on a roll, in full stride, I didn't want to stop. But, I could see she was going to talk to me and clearly, I was the person she had chosen to ask for directions.

I took my headphones out and tried a little smile. She asked me if I knew where Wilson Road was, she had been told it was closer to Southend Train Station by the person she was visiting, but someone on the train had told her Westcliff Train Station was closer to the road she was going to.

The lady had jumped off a train stop too early and then she had walked back up in the wrong direction. She had found herself amid deepest darkest Westcliff and she was headed completely the wrong way. I re-directed her, and walked alongside her, because I was headed that way, we had a little chat about all the experiences in her life which had led her here from London.

I love London, I was born there, and I worked there for years, travelling every day from Shoeburyness or Leigh or Chalkwell or Westcliff depending on where I was living, into Fenchurch Street. We had a lovely chat, and I was able to drop her off at the door where she was going. There are 250,000 approx. people in this City, of Southend on Sea, Essex, it always amazes me when I think of that statistic of how people meet each other and bump into each other, coincidentally, it hardly seems probable.

But this woman, who had been mis-directed, found me, to ask where Wilson Road was. Did I know Wilson Road? Well, not only did I used to live there, but it was where I was living when I gave birth to my only son, in 1993. The road has huge significance for me.

That sort of thing. The meaning the place has for the person being asked for directions is almost just as important as the meaning for the person who is trying to find the way!

I was in a place at the time where I was able to recognise that this lady who was asking for my directions would also enjoy the coincidence, so I shared that this is where I used to live, we both laughed and really enjoyed the moment. A gift from the Universe, not just a coincidence, but an appreciation of the wonders of the Universe bringing exactly the right people together at the right moment in time.

Being asked if you know something, being asked for information, or when you are in a supermarket, people mistake you for someone who works there. Do you know where the eggs are? Of course...I have just bought some myself, I know exactly where they are.

Being asked for information about travel, buses, trains, planes, automobiles, maybe this is something that travellers of a certain age do, they check arrangements, they double-check the information, they doubt themselves or doubt that they are looking at the right information, so they check with other humans. Maybe it is a thing we do.

Or maybe humans can sense when another human has information they need. If you are the person who has the information, naturally other people sense this and that is why they ask you.

Whatever the reason, it is a mystery how people can sense where to find information and knowledge. You are not wearing a sign 'Ask me anything, I usually have the answer' or 'Ask me when the bus is coming, I know why the bus is late' and yet people insist on dragging information out of people who do have the information.

Being Asked for Directions in Amsterdam Story

A little story, dear reader, one which is fresh in my mind about this subject. The reason this book is being published in 2023, is because I had collected my final coincidence story for this book. It happened in Amsterdam, on a weekend trip I took to see Esther

Hicks, in person, during a two-day seminar about the Law of Attraction. (www.abraham-hicks.com).

I loved the experience. I will tell that story at the end of this book, but I had some lovely coincidences while I was travelling to Amsterdam. During my trip from the UK to Amsterdam, I found myself in need of directions. I wasn't worried, or concerned, not really, I trusted the Universe that everything would work out for me, and I would make it to the seminar at the right place at the right time. I knew the worst that could happen is that I miss the seminar that I had been wanting to attend for twenty years.

Are you sitting comfortably? Then I shall begin…the seminar dates had been set by Esther's team months in advance, if not years. Long before the train companies in the UK had decided to go on strike. The seminar was due on 12th and 13th May 2023. Guess when the rail companies had decided to go on strike. 12th and 13th May 2023.

There were no trains due from Essex into London on the morning of my flight from London City Airport to Amsterdam. I chose to stay in a hotel in London, the night before I was due to fly out. It meant travelling to London a night early, staying in the airport hotel, just to make sure I was there for 6.30 am.

As I walked from the tube to the hotel, I wasn't sure which direction I should go in. It wasn't clear from google maps how to get out of the airport car park/taxi ranks/new roadways near the airport. I asked for directions from an airport security worker who just happened to be strolling past, they pointed me in the right direction, it was through a footpath which wasn't obvious from where I was standing. It was camouflaged by greenery and an overgrown hedge. I headed off, relieved to have found someone who knew the way.

I walked along the directed path, a little black cat appeared out of nowhere and wrapped itself round my legs. Seeing that little black cat gave me a feeling of added security that I was not alone. I felt confident that I was going to make my trip, find the way and not only was everything going to be okay, but I had Spirit with me, ready to offer assistance whenever I needed it.

Skip forward to arriving in Amsterdam. I had a plan. I had a pre-purchased ticket for local travel, local buses using a printed ticket and airport transfers using a QR code on an App. I had paid in advance, online, before leaving the UK. Organised, planned, perfect, right? Well, not exactly.

I hadn't allowed enough time for the airport transfer to travel all the way into central Amsterdam and another bus back out again to the venue. I also hadn't factored in the time we were delayed by heavy winds before we landed in Amsterdam. We were delayed about 45 minutes, which might still have allowed enough time if I had known where I was going and where to get the bus.

All these things take time. I also had another task to perform before getting on the airport transfer bus. I needed to queue up at a red van, under the walkway, near platform b17 to have my QR code activated. I found myself in a queue. With no internet and a guy in the red van who wouldn't activate my QR code on my App unless it was online.

While I was queueing, a young man asked me for directions. Yes, it happens to me even when I am out of my area. I clearly give off an air of looking as though I know what I am doing, and I know where I am going, like I know the way, and so people ask me the way.

This young guy turned out to be called Francesco and he had an address on his phone which wasn't familiar to me. I apologised to him and told him that buying a ticket online was cheaper than buying a ticket at the van. It was half the price. I let him go in front of me in the queue while I tried to figure out how to get a signal on my phone. Weirdly I did get a signal on my phone long enough for the van guy to be able to do whatever it was he needed to do to activate my App and hand me a paper card for travel on the local buses. I hadn't noticed where Francesco had gone.

I waited 'in line' for the bus to get out of the airport and into Amsterdam Central. I use the term loosely; it was more of a pile-on than a queue. I joined the scrum; the bus was packed. There was one spare seat that was covered up with a giant suitcase. A young lady saw me standing, clutching a pole and she offered to move her suitcase for me. I was so fortunate to be able to squeeze into the smallest of gaps between the suitcase and the seat and I plonked myself down, holding onto the suitcase for her to save it rolling into other people.

English wasn't her first language, I thanked her. She showed me her phone and asked me for directions to get to a hotel. I spoke to her in English and again, tried to explain that I was a tourist, and I could google it for her if I had internet, which seemed like intermittent access at the airport.

Looking closer at my phone I realized my settings for roaming abroad had been set to 'off'. No wonder I couldn't get google maps up. A bit of a mystery as to how I got a signal in front of the guy with the red van. While I was messing about with my phone settings, I noticed another lady watching me and looking at the person in need of directions. I asked her, in English, if she knew the way to the hotel on the young lady's phone. She spoke to the young lady in her own language, French, and they agreed she had to get off in a few stops. I loved the idea that I was able to be the link between the woman who knew the way and the young woman who needed the information.

It was my spidey senses that prompted me to put these two complete strangers together on a bus in the middle of Amsterdam. As we travelled through Amsterdam on the packed bus, it didn't pick up any more people, the bus was too full. The bus became increasingly empty as people reached their destinations.

I genuinely had no idea where I was or where I needed to go. In my head I was taking the long route to a central bus station where I was going to find a bus out again to the venue, the venue that I had to be at in about half an hour.

I had a sinking feeling that I wasn't going to make it. As I was sitting there, looking at random names of bus stops on the information screen on the bus, I remembered a conversation I overheard in a queue at the airport. One young guy was talking to his friend about the importance of local knowledge. I just caught the snippet of how they could save half an hour off their journey by going a different way and they were enjoying the importance of their 'local knowledge'. As I was sitting on the bus the idea came to me that there might need to be some out-of-the-box thinking and a shortcut. Or a cab. I wasn't sure.

While I was pondering my next move, I saw Francesco showing his phone to a woman in a flowery dress, a lady who had been chatting to the bus driver. I think she was a local who was just taking her regular route, she was standing next to the driver and she didn't seem to be laden down with suitcases, luggage or anything much, she was just there, apparently having a chat.

Flowery dress lady looked at Francesco's phone and wasn't sure whether he should be getting of the bus at this point. He was showing her the same address that he had shown me and no-one seemed to know how to get where he needed to go.

Flowery dress lady told him that she thought he needed to get off the bus. I listened to their conversation intently and I heard them mention the 'Gashouder'. Which is where I was heading. I jumped off the bus and strolled towards Francesco who was standing with his girlfriend and flowery dress lady. Just as I was about to ask them if they were going to the Gashouder, another woman walking behind me spoke to them first, she asked them if they were looking for the house of Anne Frank. They said 'no', they all shook their heads at her, and she walked off.

I said 'the Gashouder?'. They all looked optimistically at me, as if I was saying that I knew the way! They asked me, 'Do you know the way?' again, I had to apologise. I said 'No, but I have a feeling we are within walking distance, or maybe we can share a cab'.

The seminar was due to start at two o'clock and it was about 1.30 ish. Francesco's girlfriend whipped out her google maps and voila we were 2 km away. We all agreed to walk. We had a chat and a laugh, and I entertained* the young couple. *Distracted them with chat so I could keep up with their speedy pace!

One of my distractions was to chat about the Law of Attraction, naturally, they were both on board, we all have that in common and I mentioned the black cat I had seen in the UK when I had asked for directions. Francesco's girlfriend asked me if I had seen that black cat we had just walked past. I asked her if she was joking. She said no, she thought I was telling the black cat story because I had noticed the black cat sitting in a shop window. She had noticed the cat and then I started telling the story. We laughed and I enjoyed the coincidence.

This young couple were so very kind to me, slowing their pace to help me get to the venue with them. Dear Francesco and girlfriend (my apologies I have forgotten your name) if you ever read this, know that you were used by Source that day to help me. I am sorry that you found yourself off the beaten track, but I am pretty sure that you were put on my path to be able to help me. Thank you. Thanks for taking the time out of your race to the seminar to help someone else.

Another funny thing about this story is that Francesco's girlfriend was telling me that he often goes the long way, and takes a detour, the most interesting scenic route. She has spent twenty years knowing that he does this, and she has learnt not to listen to his hunches for finding himself off the beaten track.

As we walked through bicycle-strewn back streets of Amsterdam, taking as many shortcuts as google would allow, we did have a laugh about the idea that we were all on the 'wrong' bus (the long winded route) so we could meet up and they could help me make it to the venue on time.

I was reminded that when Francesco was listening to his impulses and hunches, there is more going on than we can see with our eyes. There is always a higher intelligence at work, an emotional intelligence, a spiritual intelligence. Thank you, Francesco, your kindness meant a lot.

Do you have the Time?

When was the last time someone asked you for the time? In this day and age of the mobile phone, there are still people who don't know the time, and they will find you, because you do know what time it is.

I didn't used to wear a watch. I used to lose them, I would take them off to wash my hands and leave them in random bathrooms. I also have a black cat tattoo on the inside of my left wrist which I feel looks strange having a restriction of a watchstrap. So, I don't wear a watch and yet people ask me if I know what the time is. (Although in recent years I have picked up the habit of wearing a watch again, mainly due to the step counting function).

But, the question, 'Do you have the time' is a really good question. Whenever someone asks me for the time I am pulled into the present, I take it as a sign from spirit, a nudge, that now is the time. Whatever it is that you want to do, get it done. Do not procrastinate. You never know when you are not going to have the time. Life happens. Stuff happens. If you have an idea that you are going to do something, start today, even if it is just opening a document on your computer and making a list of things you are going to do! The only time any of us have is now.

As I am writing this book, I was asked the time today. Since cellphones have a time displayed on their screens, it is becoming an ever more unusual request. Apart from acting as a reminder of the time, and how short life is, it can also act as a coincidental number. Once you have learnt to interpret life events, against the backdrop of coincidence, you will also start to notice at what time of day you are asked to check your watch. Today I was asked at 3.21. Also, a recurring number at various times in my life, a reminder of a countdown. The clock is ticking.

Present day, writing this book. Walking round the block to notch up some daily steps with my adult son (now 30). He was approached by two youngsters (late teens) asking for the time. I kid you not. What are the Chances? Currently mobile phones that have time displayed on them, people just don't need to ask the time anymore. Both my son and I found it strange. My son tends to roll his eyes whenever I mention any deeper meanings to these events. To my mind, being asked for the time is both a) a reminder that time is running out and I should get some projects finished and b) that act of being asked the time is a spiritual event. A prompt for those people to speak with my son, right in front of my eyes (I was walking behind him, we were single file on a narrow pavement) just as I am writing this paragraph in my book.

Mistaken Identity

Or being called by a different name. I hesitate to use the word 'wrong', the wrong name, because obviously, if it isn't your name, it is the wrong name, however, I don't believe you have been called the wrong name by accident. For some reason, the Universe wants to remind you of a different person. The name you have been called. Or the person doing the misnaming is being reminded of someone (often a person who has passed over to Spirit, someone who is dead).

Next time you notice this happening to you, really try and pay attention to that next step, the step of remembering a person with that name, or contacting someone you know who is still on the planet, with that name.

Fancy seeing you here!

Bumping into someone you know, even when you are miles away from home is another occurrence which leaves the people involved often scratching their heads in amazement and wonder.

Bumping into a Friend in Canada Story

I had this experience in Canada. when I was 22. I ventured off to Canada to experience what I could. A friend group had the opportunity to visit someone who had gone to live there. I wasn't the only person who went out to visit this person, a small group of friends had gone before me. I was travelling with my flatmate and her boyfriend, there were three of us, not much to worry about, but we were travelling on a wing and a prayer, the name of a town and a phone number. What could go wrong?

We had the confidence and fearlessness of youth on our side, and we found ourselves walking through the main street of a small town in Canada. One of our friends had been there for a few weeks already, but it was still a surprise to see him sitting on a wall outside a milkshake shop. He was more surprised than we were, but there he was.

Our unexpected guide was able to help show us the way and take us to our destination. We did all feel lucky that we had bumped into him. I think lucky is an understatement and I am not entirely sure what we would have done if we hadn't met him, sitting there, minding his own business at exactly that moment as we walked by.

Someone else I know travelled from Essex to Paris, France on a school trip to visit the Eiffel Tower. As he was walking up the steps, he noticed a familiar face in the crowd, coming down the steps. It was his cousin, who was also there on a school trip, from a completely different school.

To my way of thinking, that is even more of a surprising event since it wasn't 'expected' in any way from either party.

Category 3

Nature

"I go to nature to be soothed and healed, to have my senses put in order."
John Burroughs

Being in this world, we are part of nature. Mother Earth, as well as being our playground and source of life, is a Being with intelligence beyond our comprehension and we are part of the fauna and flora with which we share the planet. Mother Nature manages and organizes the weather, thunderstorms, rainbows, earthquakes, vast oceans, billowing clouds, and thousands of different types of flowers and flora with a synchronicity that is difficult to comprehend. If you spend too much time thinking about it, it can be a little mind-boggling.

All sorts of physical events take place, everything from earthquakes and crashing waves to serendipitous encounters with rocks falling in front of us, or huge chunks of ice falling from glaciers, rivers overflowing, through to the smallest sign, such as a lone ant on a car dashboard, or a bee buzzing around our head as we are thinking about making a phone call.

All of these remarkable happenings bear profound meanings, inviting us to decipher their hidden messages and glean wisdom from the intricate, interconnectedness of the natural world, of which we are a part. If a tree falls in the forest, without an ear to translate the vibration, no-one would hear it fall (www.abraham-hicks.com). Makes sense. However, just because it didn't make a sound that registered in the forest, doesn't mean that all the trees weren't aware that it happened.

I include astrology in this category, mainly because the belief that the other planets have an effect on our lives can only be categorised as natural portents. Full moon, new moon, solar eclipses, all sworn by, as omens, a sign of a good time to do…x,y or z, the solar eclipses are seen as a moment of wonder all around the world, people stop what they are doing and experience the moment. A time for universal stillness and awareness.

I haven't found enough evidence to show that all people born under the sign of Aries, for instance, are hard-headed and strong minded. The ones I know do also have a softer, gentle side and rarely say boo to a goose unless they have a bee in their bonnet and then there is no stopping them.

But aren't these personality traits so general as to be able to apply to everyone? It is this generic nature of Astrology linked to personality types which I am unable to find any consistency or absolute truth in the theory, because I also believe that personality is malleable, we change as we progress through life, our self-development and life experiences change our personalities.

Perhaps that is in keeping with where the planets are throughout our life. Of course, it is possible that self-development happens alongside the movement of the planets. Looking at astrology, I have found there are times when it seems like too much of a coincidence for it not to be a fateful timing.

The Universal Clock has ticked into place, with the planets being the markers of events which are going to happen. I have found this to be true when Mercury turns Retrograde. Two or three times a year Mercury turns Retrograde, if ever your travel plans are likely to be disrupted, it is then.

All sorts of communication errors and misunderstandings happen, air traffic controllers go on strike, train drivers refuse to do overtime. If it involves travel, computers and communication, it is almost guaranteed to go wrong or at least not go according to plan, when Mercury is Retrograde.

Jonathan Cainer (18/12/1957 – 02/05/2016) the world-famous astrologer, who sadly is no longer with us, recommended a book 'Sun of God' (Sams 2009) which is of the opinion that the earth has a self-awareness, and the Sun has consciousness.

Coincidental Star Signs Story

I also had reason to ponder about the most famous authors of Children's Literature. I was wondering about J.K. Rowling's zodiac sign, I look it up. A Leo! Of course, naturally good with children, great parents and eternally childlike themselves. Oh, and then of course another author who was criticised as much as acclaimed, Enid Blyton, a generation of children went adventuring with the Famous Five and Timmy. I wonder when she was born.

Wikipedia, what did we do before you were invented? Only to find Enid Blyton was also born under the zodiac sign of Leo. Lovely. Two Leo female writers of children's fiction grabbed the imagination of a generation. Oh, and of course, Beatrix Potter, not only a writer, but the illustrator of Peter Rabbit and

Benjamin Bunny series, I will give you three guesses as to which zodiac sign she was born under? Yes, another Leo. A trio of Leos. These were the sort of coincidental dates that kept me going as I was reading and writing about coincidence.

Death

Often people seem to die around the time of their solar return. Around the time of their birthday. It is quite common for people to die just before or after their own birthday. When the earth is in the same position in relation to the sun as it was at the time of their birth.

Occasionally, some people die on their actual birthday. For me, death isn't something to fear, but it is to be respected. There is nothing any of us can do about it. Unfortunately, I have found, particularly in the UK, people are still reticent to talk about death.

People see it as morbid, or they fear dying, or they feel they want to avoid talking about a time in the future when they no longer exist. Death becomes a much easier concept to deal with once you know that there is life after death, your Spirit, and the essence of who you are does not extinguish itself on leaving your physical body. You are eternal. You are Spirit. You came from Spirit, and you will return to Spirit.

Whatever you do whilst you are here, on the planet, is up to you. There is a rhyme and reason to life, there are no coincidences or accidents, everything happens for a reason.

The Moon

People often associate the full moon with supernatural weirdness. The dark of the moon also brings an unknown stretch for the imagination. The veil which separates our consciousness, and our higher levels of consciousness, thins during the dark of the moon, just before each new moon.

I have also found that the phases of the moon seem to have an influence on us little humans. The full moon is often shown to have a supernatural quality, particularly in the movies, Hollywood does love a full moon. The full moon is a time when earthly matters are highlighted, the need to feel human, emotionally full, loving, joyful and creative. It is often the time when women ovulate and fall pregnant. The full moon is romantic, hopeful, full of optimism for the future.

Listening to the Art Bell Radio Show, Coast to Coast, from the archives, when he used to talk about paranormal events, humans with extrasensory perceptions and in particular, remote viewing. He mentioned that a test that was carried out using remote viewers did have better results during the dark of the moon and they had less accurate images and information on the full moon.

But I believe, it is the dark of the moon which allows a clearer connection with Spirit. The time when the veil is lifted, or thinned, the best time for after-death communication, and the best time to ask for guidance from your higher self.

The dark of the moon is the best time to fast, start a new diet, a new exercise regime, and a good time to give up any addictions or unwanted behaviours. Leave them with the dark of the moon, and move into the new moon phase, seeing each day as a step closer to where you want to be.

Giving up a behaviour is hardest in the first 14 days, with the pull of the full moon creating the most difficult cravings for a few days, but then once you get over the hump of your first full moon, the rest of the way is all downhill towards the next moon phase. It is as though the full moon casts a spell over our clear thinking, our clairvoyance is clouded by the full moon.

The other argument of course, is that there is never a good time to give up something you are going to crave. You are either giving something up after the full moon, heading towards the new moon, or you are giving it up after the new moon, heading towards the full moon.

Test it for yourself and see if it makes any difference to you.

It is almost as if we are full of water, and our water is puffed up and drawn towards the full moon, making us like dew drops swaying on the petals in the early morning.

For a couple of days each month, we are all at the mercy of the moon Goddess. Although as part of our self-development and self-awareness journey, by becoming aware that this is an experience which will be happening, we are able to prepare ourselves.

Taking care of our own personal thoughts and feelings allows us to stay in control and take advantage of this knowledge so we can choose the best days for different activities. Moon sensitive people can often find themselves almost beside themselves during a full moon, you know, those days when inconveniences take on a life of their own. Keys navigate mysteriously away from their usual home, phones slip beneath sofa cushions, only to resurface three hours after turning the house upside down in a search for them.

Category 4
Animals

Understanding the meanings and beliefs surrounding animals brings us firmly into the realm of Superstition. Beginning with the black cat.

In the United Kingdom, to have a black cat cross your path is considered a lucky portent. In other countries, such as the United States, a black cat is seen as the direct opposite and is deemed unlucky. The history of Superstitions is often so deeply ingrained in Societies for generations that even in this modern day of scientifically minded, hardnosed, evidence-demanding, educated people, the long-held, handed down beliefs are often held secretly.

Animals or symbols of animals showing up in our lives. Birds, cats, dogs, all manner of fauna can hold deep significance. Sometimes animals show up to bring us messages of love, a reminder that all is well. Animals have a healing vibration and often when we are in a happy, healthy, loving place, animals come to us naturally.

Of course, there is nothing new about using an animal as a Totem, as defined by Webster's Dictionary:

"An object (such as an animal or plant) serving as the emblem of a family or clan and often as a reminder of its ancestry; also: a usually carved or painted representation of such an object"

It is not just the symbolism or beliefs we attach to animals; it is also the psychic abilities and extra sensory awareness which is peculiar to animals. Ask any animal owner who has a close relationship with their pet, animals often have an awareness and know that their owner is on the way home, even when their owner changes their normal routine.

Whether animals are changing because of their involvement with humans it is impossible to tell. Animals do seem to have a natural connection with the earth, leading them to turn tail and run, when 'sensing' the vibrations of dangers, such as tsunamis, earthquakes, and other natural disasters, they trust their instincts and head for the hills.

Some animals are more developed in one area than others, just as fish are good at swimming but not so good at climbing trees, but if you judge the intelligence of a fish by its ability to climb trees, it will live its whole life thinking it is stupid. (This statement was attributed to Albert Einstein, but even google isn't sure if Einstein actually said this!).

Some animals, like monkeys, are able to recognise themselves in a mirror, whereas most cats and dogs cannot. Dolphins are so highly socialised that they each have individual names in their pods. Personally, I would feel that if I was visited by a Dolphin, I would see if a highly spiritual gift from the Universe.

Black Cat on Halloween Story

One Halloween, I think it may have been 2015, I was a passenger with one of my friends driving along in Leigh on Sea, in Essex. Unknown territory for her, heading for an afternoon service at a spiritualist church on a Wednesday afternoon.

My friend was driving along the main road, she needed to turn right at the next turning, but she was talking and thinking about something entirely different, so she drove past the turning.

'Sorry' she said.

'Not to worry' I said, resigning myself to the idea that we were going to be driving the long way round to double-back on ourselves and get back to the right road, and we were probably going to be late.

As we drove down the unplanned route, we both saw a giant white lorry parked across the bottom of the street. On the side of the lorry was a picture of a giant black cat! I shook my head in disbelief. We both enjoyed a laugh. The wrong turning was clearly meant to happen so we could see the giant picture of the Black Cat on Halloween.

Just to reinforce the idea, for you, dear reader, of how much I love the sign of the Black Cat, I do have a tattoo of a black cat on my left wrist. It is my thing, my favourite symbol. So, personally, I felt blessed, rewarded in some way, by the Universe.

Feathers

Another common messenger from the Universe, is the feather. The common garden variety, yes, of course, and the more exotic or even fake feathers can show up when you most need it.

Having a feather appear in your world, whether it is because you are walking amongst pigeons or whether you are indoors in an entirely feather-free zone, I feel the feathers are brought to us to remind us of the importance of being spiritual. As well as comforting us to let us know we are not alone, they can also point to a decision to be made and you are being asked to choose the spiritual path. You may also be asked to act as an earth Angel. Someone may ask for your help or you may spot a chance to be able to offer your help before being asked.

Feathers don't always show up in the freshly plucked from the bird variety, sometimes fake feathers show up, all sorts of colours, sometimes stuck on a hat or a feather boa! Be prepared for your feathers to show up in whatever shape your Guardian Angel sees fit.

When feathers show up, I see it as a notification from Spirit that our Guardian Angels are drawing near. Why this is happening, is for you to interpret. Feathers showing up in unexpected places is one of my favourite things, you know, strolling into the library, not thinking about feathers at all, only for a feather to fall out of a book you pick up.

This happened to me, during a time when I was reading signs from the Universe by interpreting what I called Suburban Symbols, you know, when written words, text in all forms, shows up in random places. So, I was noticing symbols, but I wasn't looking for the feather, and yet there it was, sitting on the page of a book I opened in the library, and the feather floated to the floor. I think this is one of the most common ways our Guardian Angels communicate with us. Feathers fall to our feet when there are no birds about.

Feathers blow across our paths, fall on our heads, show up in the most unlikely of places and I suspect that most people out there with an interest in Spirit, have had the experience of at least one white feather appearing on their path.

While I am here, talking of white feathers, I am reminded of a beautiful tarot reader on Youtube who I am quickly going to recommend. 'White Feather Tarot' on Youtube. She offers some uncanny words of wisdom and some amazing readings.

Feathers in the Cathedral Story

I was taking an exam towards my degree with the Open University and I had an hour to kill before the exam, it was raining cats and dogs, absolutely hammering it down, so I took advantage of seeking solace in the local church which really was more like a cathedral. As I sat in the inner sanctum, I looked down at my feet and saw I was surrounded by feathers, three or four large feathers had appeared, I hadn't noticed them when I sat down, but they gave me comfort and strength to take the exam, which I did go on to pass.

Feather on a Foot Story

One of my friends, bear with me dear reader, I have pestered my friends for coincidence stories as I have been putting this book together, one of my friends went to the funeral of one of his close friends, a man in his thirties, in Scotland, still part of the United Kingdom, as I write this.

My friend flew from London to Scotland for the funeral. As he stepped from the plane, a feather floated onto his foot, he felt that was a sign from his friend that he was okay and that he was aware of my friend's effort to make his funeral.

Birds bring meanings, messages, signs, omens of good news, bad news, births, deaths and marriages.

You know the rhyme about magpies? One for sorrow, two for joy, three for a girl, four for a boy, five for silver, six for gold, seven for a secret never to be told.

Crows are messengers of news. Which may be wanted or unwanted, If I hear a crow crowing, I think 'I'm going to have something to crow about'. The more crows, the more there is to crow about. I have often noticed four crows showing up just before a massive change, or upheaval, such as a house move.

Flocks of birds flying overhead can symbolise a wedding. Maybe not yours, but you can expect to hear news of a wedding, or if you are lucky, an invitation to a wedding.

A solitary seagull is a symbol of freedom and independence. A reminder to be grateful for both.

Peacock Story

One of my friends had a lovely experience with a peacock in the aftermath of her dad's death. Within a couple of weeks of her dad dying, my friend was sitting in the living room of her mum's house only to see a peacock appear in the garden, out of nowhere, there were no peacocks in that area, naturally, and my friend had no idea where the peacock came from or where he vanished to, but she accepted it as a sign from her recently departed dad that all was well.

Seeing a picture of an animal can also bring a message from your higher self. It doesn't always come in the form of the actual animal; it is the symbolism which is the key.

Blue feathers story

I was on holiday in Sardinia in 2022, if you ever get a chance to go there, I would highly recommend it. White beaches, clear seas, beautiful people. It was amazing. The area I was in was rich in flora and fauna and all manner of insects that I had never seen before. Beautiful birds, cats, random dead snakes, you name it, Sardinia seems to have it. I had a few coincidences from nature while I was there.

I saw a black cat cross my path, which was unexpected, and I loved the reminder of Spirit. The next day I was up early watching the sunrise, my holiday companion was still asleep and I had ventured out in search of coffee and to enjoy the sight of the beautiful mountains and beaches. I found it breathtaking every time I looked at it. I was loving it.

As I was standing by the hotel pool, a bird flew down and landed on the back of a chair. It was quite a big bird with brown and blue feathers. It sat there and looked at me. I nodded at it and I took a photo. It sat there long enough for me to do that. I was really drawn to how blue the feathers were.

That evening I was on a tour bus, being driven through the winding mountain roads, our destination a bustling evening market.

The bus was filled with people who didn't speak English and the air was full of excitable Italian. After a lovely evening of exploring the best that Sardinia has to offer by way of tourist tat, back on the bus, having enjoyed the experience, but also looking forward to making it safely back to the hotel in the pitch black. It was a little nerve wracking.

As we were driving back, suddenly there was a huge commotion in the bus. An Italian lady was jumping in the aisle, waving her arms about wildly. I saw this little dragonfly style insect, which was a bright blue colour.

It flew away from her windmill arms that she was whirling through her hair, clearly she was convinced that it had got caught in her hair. The insect landed on the headrest directly in front of my face.

It just sat there, the whole of the return journey back to the hotel, I was accompanied by some sort of blue dragonfly. I thought it was unusual at the time.

On my return to England, I found a letter on my doormat. The letter brought me news of a death. My mum's sister, my aunty Chris had died while I was on holiday in Sardinia. Now, I see that blue feathered bird and the blue insect as being a message from my aunty Chris, a little goodbye.

Category 5
People

Parallel lives. The wonderful experience where the Universe is using people as vessels to create a set of inexplicable, unexplainable, and frankly improbable set of events. Parallel lives are those in which separate individuals, unrelated people, who share extreme similarities in their lives. They have made similar choices for the names of their spouses, their children, the cars they have purchased, the career paths they have followed. These lives are sometimes uncovered by chance meetings between the pair, but more often, because of mistaken identity.

Doppelgangers are also becoming more known. I use these words carefully, because of course, years ago, we had no idea of any Doppelgangers, but with the advent of the internet and websites such as 'twinstrangers.net', allows any of us to search for our double. There are now stories on the internet pretty much daily, of people who look like each other, sitting next to each other on planes, trains and in traffic queues.

Laura Buxton Story

The story of Laura Buxton and her pink balloon. When Laura Buxton was 10 years old, a little girl, with long brown hair, she tied her name and address to a pink balloon and let it off. It flew across the country and landed in the garden of another 10-year-old girl, also with long brown hair, also called Laura Buxton. The parents of the two girls made contact, the girls made friends, they also discovered they both had three year old golden retrievers at home.

Deepak Chopra Book Story

One of my favourite synchronicity stories involve a fantastic writer, up there with the best of them, Deepak Chopra. I find his words are easy to read and a joy. He does have a fan base and people do tend to look out for his works as and when they appear in book shops.

Deepak had a new book out and he was flying somewhere to publicise the book. As he was leaving the country and taking a long-haul flight, his publicist had driven him to the airport and insisted that Deepak take a copy of his latest book with him on the plane.

Deepak knew that there would be hundreds of his book available at his destination, he didn't really need to be taking the book with him, but he signed the copy and stuffed it into his carry-on bag.

Sitting on the plane, Deepak was listening to his fellow passenger, seated next to him, talking about his work and what he did for a living and then he asked Deepak what he did. Deepak says he is an author.

'Oh' the passenger remarked. 'My wife wants me to pick her a book up from the airport on my way through. There is a book out that she wants, by someone called Deepak Chopra'.

Deepak reached into his bag and pulled the book out. 'This one?' He handed the book to the newly jaw-dropped passenger. Not only had he saved him a trip to purchase a book, but he now had a signed copy.

When people are used as a vessel of coincidence, often it is in looking back we can unravel our role and our behaviour in the unexpected sequence of events.

It does take practice to be operating 'in the moment', like Deepak, firstly, he was willing to go along with the insistence of his publisher, secondly, he struck up conversation with a complete stranger, thirdly he had the presence of mind to be aware of the book and the passenger and to piece the puzzle pieces together in order to create an extraordinary moment in time.

Chance Encounter

When and how people meet is a permanent source of fascination. How did you meet? It is a common question to a couple who are then able to reminisce and share their romantic nostalgia, rekindling the early feelings of love and romance. People often spend a lot of time analysing how they met, what happened to 'cause' the meeting. What had to happen for them to have met, and this is where people see the meeting not as coincidence but as fate, not as synchronicity or a lining up of the perfectly matched, but as Destiny.

Phoenix Rising Story

I was on Facebook, having joined a group for people interested in mediumship, being Facebook, there were people from all over the country in this little group. One guy on there mentioned his book, 'Phoenix Rising', and he explained his interest in coincidence and how Jane Seymour had often shown up in his life experience.

Naturally, I was interested, this being one of my favourite subjects. He offered to send me a copy of his book. I was grateful, he was sending me a copy for free. He sent the hardback book, unfortunately, it didn't arrive. I didn't get it! What a pain.

Put yourself in his position. Would you have gone out of your way, twice, for a stranger who expressed an interest in your book? Not many people would or feel a desire to. But this guy did, he sent another copy,

I received the second copy and sat down to read it straight away. Determined to appreciate the effort the guy had made, because, who does that? As I was reading the book, I could identify with a lot of what he had written, how following the signs and recognising when a sign was from Spirit and not ignoring the coincidences, pretty much all the same understanding I had throughout my own life.

When I reached the page about the author being related to William Pitt, the Prime Minister of England, I felt a cold chill creep across my shoulders. I could not believe what I was reading. I too am related to William Pitt, the Prime Minister of England! Turns out we are cousins. Our grandparents were sisters. What are the chances?

Nothing was stopping him from sending me that book. It was meant to be for us to find each other amongst literally millions of people on Facebook.

18th May Story

Well, the synchronicity continues. This time a couple of years ago (ish) I blogged about a guy from the ONS, (Office for National Statistics). A guy called Colin who showed up and asked me some questions. I don't mind doing surveys for people knocking on doors. I know how hard that job is. It wasn't Colin last year, it was someone who looked like Colin, talked like Colin, similar age and manner.

In my first year in this flat Colin called, he was a friendly, charming, conversationalist so I was more than happy to answer questions as to whether my teenage son considers himself British or English and if he is still a Jedi.

I was working as a self-employed eBay Shop owner selling gifts at the time. Shortly after Colin's visit I closed the eBay shop because it wasn't making enough profit. 18th May was the day I shut up shop. I was also blogging about the synchronicity that shows up in my life and how I love to spot the patterns of numbers, dates and names that show up regularly.

A year later a guy called George, also from the ONS, showed up, he had been trained by Colin, so we had a nice, easy discussion about life in general and what is going on for me. I also mentioned my interest in coincidences, and he asked me the date for my shop closing, when he said his birthday was 18th May, we both had a laugh. Something significant for him. I could have chosen any day in May to end the accounts for that eBay shop. It amazes me how these coincidences transpire.

So, here we are, 2011 and the ONS are due. The knock at the door brings a guy who is one of the above two, I say 'Are you Colin or are you the other one?' because I honestly can't tell the difference. Colin gives me a wry smile and asks if now is a good time for an interview.

'Yes, of course, although I have had flu over the weekend and I wouldn't want you to catch anything' I tell him, because I wouldn't want to expose him to my germs.

Off he goes to collect his computer from the car, because he didn't know if I was going to be in, giving me time to 'tidy', ie dump my duvet that I had been lounging around in to get well quicker, back in my bedroom and open a window to freshen my pit up.

Colin comes back and we settle down to our regular annual check-up. He does explain that George is no longer. Colin interviewed George, told him to apply for a job, trained him and shared the Southend area with him. So, when my address came up as time for annual review Colin phoned George to find out why he wasn't doing it, since George had been assigned to me.

George's son answered the phone. 'Sorry, George isn't available, he died half an hour ago'. Poor Colin. What are the chances of deciding to phone someone to speak to them just after they have died. I do not believe in coincidences. I am pretty sure that this did not happen by chance. Colin was guided to make the call to find out about George, probably by George. It is bizarre that Colin heard of George's death pretty much as soon after it happened, when he hadn't had reason to speak with George for more than six months. The person he was calling about was me.

Well, when Colin asked me if anything has changed? meaning my work situation or marriage status or religious beliefs I told him that the only thing that has changed is the interviewer has died. We both had a good laugh. You have to laugh. Of course, death is no laughing matter, but sometimes the absurdity of life is simply laughable.

I probably won't be seeing Colin again, he will be retiring in 5 months, I will not be seeing George again, he died of a heart attack in his early sixties. After walking his wife home from the theatre, puffing a bit, he sat down and died. Just like that. A life is snuffed out. Gone, but not forgotten.

Names

The power that a name has when we identify with someone, is difficult to explain, isn't it? Clearly, we all understand the feelings that come up when we hear the name of a loved one, either in Spirit or someone who is still alive. Maybe I could have had a category purely for the subject of names, since this is the most obvious 'message' that comes from Spirit, particularly at church, or through mediums. If they get the name right, you feel as though they have linked up with Spirit.

If people mention their pets to me, I do tend to ask the name of the pet 'What was your dog called?' or the cat, or the budgie, of the aunty or uncle, whoever or whatever it was they have mentioned. It does open up a space for the Universe to deliver a coincidence.

This is just my experience, and it is just what happens for me. Don't take my word for it, try it for yourself. It reminds me of the time I was walking along in Southend, with a friend, who has a grandson called Monty. A man walked towards us with a puppy, naturally we both made a fuss of the puppy and I asked his name. 'Monty' the man said. We both enjoyed the coincidence.

As I was editing this book I was talking with a friend about a cat they had, the cat was called Alice. He said that he saw the name Alice all the time, mainly, he thought, because Alice in Wonderland shows up regularly everywhere. I honestly couldn't remember the last time google bought up a picture of Alice in Wonderland for me. Nor could I really think of anyone who had ever shown up in my life who was called Alice. I guessed it was that thing where you only notice the names that have meaning for you.

A few weeks later I was sitting in a coffee shop that doubles up as a second-hand book shop, run by volunteers. I was listening to a friend talking and as we sat there, my attention was drawn to a shelf of books behind her. You know what I am going to say, dear reader, there was an 'Alice in Wonderland' book, and it was in pride of place on top of the bookshelf. It wasn't where you would have expected it to be though, it wasn't in the children's section, or even the fiction section, it was in the travel section. Maybe someone was having a laugh or taking the 'Land' bit literally.

Naturally, I took a photo and shared it with the person who had spoken to me about the name Alice. We both enjoyed the coincidence. A few weeks later, just before I was heading to Amsterdam for my weekend extravaganza, I decided to advertise my car for sale on Gumtree. I had been thinking about trading up for a while, but I just decided to put an advert on. Do I need to tell you, dear reader, the name of the person who contacted me about buying my car? That's right, Alice.

Category 6

Physical Feedback

Our bodies are incredible when you stop for a second to think about it. All the tasks our bodies perform for us and we barely give it a second thought, you know, like renewing our skin, keeping our lungs breathing. Our body doesn't like to bother us with unnecessary information. It just gets on with the job. Sometimes however, our body does try to get our attention when it senses something that our conscious self isn't aware of. Our body sends us emotional messages. We receive the message in the form of a hunch, intuition, a gut feeling. Heightened sensing from your body can be a very powerful tool to keep us safe and also for all sorts of other information gathering. Intuition can prove really helpful in dangerous situations; our inner gut feelings can prevent us from walking any further into the path of danger. Practicing using our intuitive ability as often as possible will help to strengthen this ability.

How do you do that? Well, you can practice by taking a daily walk. Being aware of your surroundings, noticing the events which happen around you, following your instincts, which will heighten just by being outdoors in nature, fresh air, natural sunlight, having birds around, neighbourhood animals and a sense of feeling on purpose.

Do it on purpose, allow yourself to be guided by your own inner self, your inner sense of knowing is lying dormant, latent, if you will, to be called upon when/if you should need it. Why not get used to waking it up early? Let it out, trust it, trust your own inner guidance system.

Interpreting Messages from Your Body

Our body is the vehicle of our soul, when our inner spirit, our inner being, our actual soul is being ignored, kept in the dark, avoided, not dealt with, however you want to say that you are out of touch with your inner sense of knowing, the pain erupts into physical ailments.

There are many books on the subject of how to interpret the needs from your own physical body, for instance, in a metaphysical sense, what does it mean to have a pain in your back? Relating that back to your experience of the physical realm, maybe you are in need of support in your day-to-day life.

Generally speaking, pain we feel on the inside is often as a result of something occurring on the outside which we do not want. Something unwanted, unasked for, not requested or desired, appearing in our reality, our external, material world. This is often something which we also feel we have no control over.

Your body is bringing you messages about changes it would like to see in your life, either your lifestyle or particularly if you are out of balance in terms of level of activity, exercise or diet or the amount of time you are spending with your family or at work.

Physical Events inside the home

There are many Universal Laws which govern our little human lives, many of these Laws go unnoticed, unrecognized and sometimes unacknowledged. One of the Laws that has gained traction recently and has grown in popularity, is the Law of Attraction.

According to the Law of Attraction, when we have feelings which are unpleasant and therefore unwanted, it is because we are focusing our minds on unwanted aspects of the situation. We are not seeing the situation as our own Inner Being, or, our Spiritual Self, sees it. We are not choosing to paint the picture the same way Source is viewing it. The way to help ourselves is to recognise where we are throwing the proverbial spanner into our own works.

Sometimes we literally fall flat on our face in public, or take a stumble or a trip, or we have a near miss, saving ourselves at the last minute from what could have been a nasty fall. Our Inner Self is asking us to take care of our next life step. No matter whether it is changing jobs, having a new relationship, moving house, changing phone provider or finding a tradesman, pay attention to how you feel about the new set of circumstances. Is it really the best direction for you to take? Is it the path of least resistance?

Messages from our higher intelligence don't just come to us when we are outside our own home. Many actions from within the home reflect exactly what is going on for us either in our emotional experience, our relational status or our latest life events.

When people are focusing on their physical material existence, with no regard to the meaning of their life or spiritual experience, often the Universe tries to break through by creating a bit of drama or chaos in our daily lives. Some of these Universal nudges can be stronger than others. Some houses will require workmen to call, and a bit of plastering will sort it out, and some houses will have deep cracks uncovered which will need foundations digging up, both states reflect the state of the house owner.

How many times have you known people with a divorce looming discover half a dozen problems with the house they are selling? You know the old adage; It never rains but it pours. People often say that it always happens at once, but this usually isn't strictly true. By paying attention to the small creaks and cracks will lead to protection and possibly prevention from the larger breakdowns.

It may seem like common sense to people who have passed through their own levels of understanding of life, the practical nature of maintaining a home, looking after electrical goods such as washing machines and cookers, it is part of life, and the metaphysical is for analysis and understanding on a personal level.

Take washing machines for example, they last on average, with average use 4-5 years? Assuming no abuse and they are cleaned regularly, maintained regularly, using tablets to remove the limescale, some sort of water softener, so everyone can expect their washing machines to last the same amount of time. Right? Makes sense, it is logical, practical, reality, the facts. But the truth, the reality, the actual facts are that there is no exact measurement or understanding as to why one person's washing machine lasts for 18 months and their next-door neighbour's machine lasts for 40 years. It is in the analysis though, of events which happen to appliances in the home, which act as a mirror for us to know where we can change our thoughts, feelings or behaviours to improve our own lining up with the universe.

Some of you will already be aware of the regularity of lightbulbs popping, computers grinding to a halt, irons packing up, kettles refusing to play, fuses blowing and all manner of electrical fails. Electrical disturbances are usually analogous to thought disturbances, stress, negative thinking and generally asking you to check your thoughts.

Also, needing works to be carried out in the home may bring you to a shop where you have to buy the replacement items, pay attention to words which are spoken to you, pay attention to all the interactions, the journey to the shop, the choice of item. As you tell the story to people about the event, pay attention to the words you use and the words which are spoken back to you. The Universe, your Higher Self, your Spirit Guides are all trying to get your attention or pass you a message.

Another vehicle for metaphysical messages is from our car, mechanical problems, punctures, oil leaks, anything in need of repair can easily be translated into the metaphysical.

Water-related issues and disturbances such as leaks, relate to our emotional states.

Category 7
Inanimate Objects

When coincidence touches us from beyond the grave using inanimate objects.

The inanimate object only holds meaning because it is linked to a human being. A person, without whose identity, consciousness and life experience there would be no coincidence.

Have you noticed random objects showing up in your life, repeatedly? This literally could be any object that you can think of. People have all sorts of things, like, pennies, lightbulbs, forks, all the usual small things like lighters, keys, articles of clothing and then there are larger, less likely, less expected objects show up.

I went through a phase of seeing sets of silver ladders on my path. Both outside buildings and inside buildings, ladders blocking my path as well as being brought into my home. Objects around which there is a coincidence. For me, at the time, I saw the silver ladders as a reminder that there is room for spiritual growth, taking steps up the silver ladder, like moving closer to heavenly realms. I still love seeing silver ladders.

Sometimes inanimate objects are seemingly used by the Universe to bring messages to us. These can range from the way a plastic bag is blown in the wind, only to land at our feet, through to having a piano abandoned on our path.

All things great and small, have meaning in the Universe. Whether they are made of plastic, silk, wood, metal or any other material which has manifested from the spiritual. Although the items are inanimate, they carry messages for us to interpret.

It is our own personal interpretation of the items which bring personal meaning to the event of seeing objects on our travels. My particular favourites are the objects which show up in unexpected places.

Green Glass Charm Story

Around the end of the '90s I used to carry a lucky charm with me. It was made of glass; it was rectangular shaped, dark green with a four-leaf clover etched on in a lighter shade of green. It was about the size of two thumbnails. Yes, if you put your thumbs side by side, that is how big it was. I was carrying it for luck, or comfort, or to help me to feel reassured. I had a deep belief in things that you cannot see, not a superstition, more of a knowing. For me, the little charm in my pocket was a reminder of the spiritual nature of life.

One day, c2000, I was racing along in Southend-on-Sea, clutching the hand of my seven-year-old son as we tore through busy streets. I was wearing a denim jacket and I put my four-leaf clover, green stone in the top left pocket.

Suddenly I noticed the green stone in the road, down by the side of the kerb. I couldn't understand for a minute what had happened to my lucky charm. I wondered if somehow it had fallen out of my pocket. I couldn't see how that had happened. I hadn't bent over for any reason.

I patted my jacket pocket and felt the familiar lump of the glass stone in my pocket. I reached down and picked the stone up. It was an identical green stone, with a four-leaf clover etched on it. I gave one of the stones to my son and for a while we both took to carrying them around, knowing that we both had a connection through the stones. What are the chances? An identical shape, colour, identically decorated, glass stone.

Red Seat Ibiza Story

Seat Ibiza coincidence. I was succeeding with my Law of Attraction experiment in that I 'asked' or 'ordered' something unexpected, within 48 hours.

I had bid on a car on eBay which I wasn't expecting to

win because of the low value of my bid. I was also in the middle of negotiating with a main car dealer over the price of a little run around, more expensive, but newer. In the middle of my manifested holiday to Malta I heard that I had won the bright red Seat Ibiza! Wow! What a turn up. Oh dear. Two cars due to be on my hands.

When I returned from holiday, I met someone who knew someone who might be interested in buying my little red Seat from me. That link-up was a coincidence, it was the husband of a friend's sister. My friend came round with her husband, they test drove the car in the dark, in the rain, we took it to the petrol station, they were happy with it and they made me an offer. I happily accepted because I needed the parking space and they seemed to really enjoy the car as well. They explained that she had another sister, in Romania who had an identical car, a red Seat Ibiza! I watched the car drive away knowing that I won it on eBay so it could be passed on to the owner it was destined for!

Anthony Hopkins Book Story

The actor, Anthony Hopkins had just been offered the leading role in a film based on the book, 'The Girl from Petrovka'. He traipsed around book shops in London, trying to find a copy of the book. Unsuccessful, he set off for home.

As he waited for the train, he noticed a book lying on a bench. On closer inspection he discovered it was the exact book that he had been searching for.

It was a dog-eared copy of 'The Girl from Petrovka'. He pocketed the book and kept it for his research for the film he was about to star in.

Two years later, he was on set, filming in Vienna, when the writer of the book appeared, George Feifer. As they were chatting about the film, the writer mentioned that he didn't even have a copy of his own book. The last one he had been using, with annotations in the margins, his working copy, had been lost somewhere in London, by a friend he had lent it to.

Anthony Hopkins handed George the book he had found, 'Is this the one?' Anthony asked, 'With the notes scribbled in the margins?'. It was the same book.

The gloves are off

I thought it was just me who liked to notice when random gloves turn up on my path. Literally on the path that I am walking on, I will see a glove, or a pair of gloves, lost, abandoned, separated from the matching one, that is until Tom Hanks started sharing pictures of lost gloves on his jogging path. The world sits up and takes notice when Tom Hanks points out random items.

When I see gloves on my path I take it as a sign that the hard work has been done. Now you can take a rest. Ease up, relax, chill, meditate. Wait. Wait and see what shows up from the Universe.

Hats off to you

Have you ever noticed how many hats are lying around? People drop hats a lot. This happens more in hat season, during the autumn, when people have forgotten that they were wearing a hat, or something. I have never lost a hat, so I don't really know what people would be thinking when they lose one.

There is absolutely no point in me asking you, dear reader, 'What you were thinking when you lost a hat?', because then you wouldn't have lost it, would you? Unless of course, it fell off into a place that was impossible to access. Like on a roller coaster ride.

Since I notice hats a lot in Autumn and then again in Spring, I am taking it that it could be something to do with the weather. But as I do also see hats all year round, it doesn't explain every hat on my path.

I see a hat as a pat on the back from Spirit. A little boost, a reminder from Spirit that you have Spirit Guides paying attention to your every move, thought, feeling and action.

A fork in the road

Or a fork in your path? Have you noticed a dropped fork on the pavement? I take this as a symbol that you have a choice of two paths, a fork in the road. A fork shows up. A definite choice to make which will feel like a decision. The choice to be made may seem like a straightforward choice to onlookers and to people on the outside of the situation, but for the person who has to make the choice, the factors can seem quite complex, otherwise the decision wouldn't feel like a decision, it would seem like the natural flow of life. When a fork shows up, the choices will lead to vastly different outcomes.

Wizard of Oz Story

This following story was dismissed as a publicity stunt, but reading this version on Snopes fact checker site, I like to believe it happened:

Quote:

What definitely did occur on The Wizard of Oz (written by L. Frank Baum) – perhaps the most astonishing thing that did occur – was dismissed as a publicity stunt. Yet it is vouched for by [cinematographer] Hal Rosson and his niece Helene

Bowman and by Mary Mayer, who served briefly as the unit publicist on the picture.

'For Professor Mayer's coat', says Mary Mayer, 'They wanted grandeur gone to seed. A nice-looking coat but very tattered. So the wardrobe department went down to an old second-hand store on Main Street and bought a whole rack of coats. And Frank Morgan and the wardrobe man and [director] Victor Fleming got together and chose one. It was kind of a Prince Albert coat. It was black broadcloth and it had a velvet collar, but the nap was all worn off the velvet.' Helene Bowman recalls the coat as 'ratty with age, a Prince Albert jacket with a green look'.

The coat fitted Morgan and had the right look of shabby gentility, and one hot afternoon Frank Morgan turned out the pocket. Inside was the name 'L.Frank Baum'.

'We wired the tailor in Chicago', says Mary Mayer, 'and sent pictures. And the tailor sent back a notarised letter saying that the coat had been made for Frank Baum. Baum's widow identified the coat too, and after the picture was finished we presented it to her. But I could never get anyone to believe the story'.

Unquote

See a penny, pick it up, and all day long you will have good luck

Wayne Dyer turned me on to the idea of asking the Universe for actual money, physical coins and notes, in the real world. Not just a promise of money at some vague time in the future, or a hope that our incomes will increase or improve in some way, but actual cash. Right here, today, right now. Every day.

I watched a Wayne Dyer talk where he explained that he never used to stoop for money as small as a dime, or in the case of the UK, a penny. Until he changed his appreciation for all the gifts the Universe was bestowing on him. I may have just put those words in his mouth, but he did say something about asking the Universe for a demonstration of abundance, daily, and so every day the coins would show up.

Wayne would not only notice them and appreciate them, but he picked them up, collected them and saved them, in a jar, hidden in a closet, no-one knew he was storing them away until he decided to abandon all of his material objects!

So, it is to this end, I too have made a commitment to enjoying receiving money from the Universe daily. Whenever I see a penny, I pick it up, take a photo, post it to Facebook, thank the Universe for the 'offering' and know that the flow of abundance, which is coming to me, isn't happening by accident.

Finding Coins in Amsterdam Story

Another story, dear reader, about my little trip to Amsterdam in 2023 to attend a Law of Attraction Seminar with Abraham-hicks. During one of the breaks, I found myself sitting alongside a newfound seminar companion. A lady who was staying in the hotel room next door to mine. I had met her the previous night, in the hotel corridor.

At the Abraham-hicks seminar we were given a pink bracelet for ID to get back into the venue. This lady and I had identified each other as Abrahamsters because of our pink bracelets. I was just flying back into my hotel room, and she was ready to go down for dinner. I told her I would be down in a minute. I rushed indoors and dumped my bag and stuff, turned round and flew down to the restaurant where she was sitting on her own with a drink. There were three other women in the restaurant, all sitting alone, all wearing their pink bracelets.

I gathered them together and invited them to join us for dinner. Before we knew it, there were five of us eating together and chatting like old friends. It was amazing and I loved the experience. The next morning, I caught up with the same woman at breakfast time and we walked back to the seminar on the second day. On the way, walking past a beautiful pond and a lovely park filled with nature, she spotted a wallet in the grass. It had clearly been discarded. It didn't have any cash in it, but it was full of ID and bank cards. I was surprised that she found it, I hadn't spotted it, I was too busy wondering at the woodpeckers and a random heron in the nearby water.

When we arrived back at the venue, she handed the wallet in, and I am sure that the staff there will have reunited the wallet with the owner or done whatever it is that you do with lost and found wallets in Amsterdam. It was this lady that I was sitting with during the break.

We were both appreciating the beautiful sunny day that we had been blessed with and shared our coincidence stories. She also had lots of lovely experiences to share. As we were sitting there, she glanced down and noticed a coin on the floor. It was a coin that neither of us were familiar with, it was a lovely reminder for both of us of the penny stories that Esther-hicks tells, as well as Wayne Dyer, and for me, personally, I loved the coin just seemingly showing up. Like I say, I was too busy looking around at all the beautiful sights to notice a coin on the floor, but my newfound like-minded friend, was observant enough to have her attention drawn. We both enjoyed the coincidence.

It isn't about the denomination, the technical value of the coin. It is what the coin represents to the person who notices it. Money on our path had meaning for both of us and we did both enjoy the moment. I have moved on from picking up coins, now I just take a photo and leave the coin for someone who needs it. But I might just start picking them up for a charity pot.

As I edit this portion of the book, I took a trip to my local library, to print out a final version, ready to edit. This task leads me to a print station in Southend library, in Essex, where my attention is drawn to a coin reflecting the light, a shiny, copper penny, on the floor at my feet. I mentally thank the Universe, I notice the penny, I pick it up, I take a photo for Facebook.

I do love to share the evidence of coincidence in my reality, and I enjoy using photographic evidence as a way to keep a record, which is just one way to do that, keeping a diary or a journal, or a blog or vlog would be just as effective. Since I have handed my financial woes over to the Universe, I have had unexpected benevolence bestowed upon me by way of a tax rebate, which was completely out of the blue. I have found pennies, and the money which I have been given in change has been of the new variety, brand new fivers, brand new coins.

I have been given money-saving tips from people, tips about how to find the best value for money. I have paid people over and above what they are expecting, hoping that as I treat people with value and respect, this is how

I will be treated by other people.

I have been as generous as I have been able to be. I have bought people coffee, handed change to homeless people whenever I have had the change, helped people whenever I have found myself in a position to do so. I think the subject of money showing up could well have a book all by itself, never mind a chapter within a category, but here we are. I had to draw the line somewhere and I gave myself a deadline.

How many times, deal lovely reader have you found yourself in desperate need of cash, only to find the exact amount you need suddenly appear on your path? It can't happen every day to everyone, but I suspect it happens every day to someone.

Unexpected Cash Story

Are you sitting comfortably? Well, during the pandemic I was working as a covid tester. This involved booking appointments with people, driving to their homes, doing the covid tests, dropping the tests to a courier who would then drive them to the labs for testing.

I had a couple of anti-synchronicity days which involved an issue at a petrol station where I used my bank card three times. One petrol pump, I put my card in, there was no petrol.

The second pump I put my card in and there was a glitch between the cashier and the pump. A button had to be pressed to allow payment at the pump and I didn't realise. I took my card out of the machine, the cashier pressed the button, I made a third attempt.

Well, I also hadn't realized, that a third attempt to use a bank card at a petrol station is highly suspect and my bank automatically froze my bank card. On a Saturday.

I had no access to cash; limited petrol and a household who were expecting me to visit them about 40 miles away near Harlow. I wouldn't normally do visits in Harlow, from Leigh. Someone who lives in Harlow would do them. However, on this day, the covid tester for that area was off sick, so I had been drafted in to cover their visits.

I drove to Harlow, explaining to the family who I was testing, what had happened. They were the nicest family. They just so happened to be the sort of family who keep spare petrol in their garage, in a metal petrol can. What are the Chances?

They lent me their spare petrol can filled with petrol in case I needed it. I felt a bit better. If I ran out of petrol, I would use their petrol in an emergency. I didn't want to have to use it. I wanted to return it to them next time I was passing through Harlow (which would probably happen at some stage in the next week, once I had my bank card working again).

I drove off, heading for Langdon Hills, another household, more covid tests. I didn't bore them with the story of my bank card or the petrol situation, I did my job and prepared to drive off.

As I was driving away, I noticed a piece of paper blowing along the road. Langdon Hills is a beautiful clean area, not the sort of place where you would expect to see random litter, particularly during the pandemic, there weren't that many people about to leave litter.

The paper turned and twisted in the wind, and I caught a glimpse of purple, what? I stopped my car, jumped out and caught the paper. It wasn't paper, it was a twenty-pound note. Yes, honestly, that happened. Just when I needed it most, the Universe delivered. I drove to the nearest petrol station, and put some petrol in.

I returned the petrol can to the Harlow family the following week. They loved the coincidence of the twenty-pound note as well. It was an unbelievable thing to happen, but happen it did. I thanked the Universe and thoroughly enjoyed the experience.

It is not the first time a cash amount has literally fallen at my feet, but never during such a precise moment of need.

Category 8
Spiritual

'Whenever you hear or read anything of a spiritual nature that moves you or touches your soul, you are not learning something…you are remembering what you have always known. It is a gentle awakening' – Unknown (A Wild Woman's Soul on Facebook)

'Hand of God' Book Story

Personally, I had a book fling itself off the shelf in the library. A heavy book which landed with a thud. Sometimes the title is apt for your current situation or provides guidance that you are looking for.

I was in a library in Wickford in Essex once, in the middle of a situation which could only be described as dire, no matter which way you looked at it, there didn't seem to be any easy way out. As I was looking for something, anything, to take my mind off my current situation there was a loud thud near a shelf full of heavy books. The thud was so loud in the quiet library, I couldn't ignore it. Although at that time I wasn't really into metaphysical interpretations or analysing my personal environment to see what sort of vibrations I was giving off.

I was just living through my life and creating by default, there was no awareness on my part of how I had control over my feelings or my thoughts. I had just moved into the giving up smoking stage.

So, to experience a physical manifestation, apparently out of the blue, led me to believe I had experienced something spooky. I believed something in Spirit, like a ghost, or my Guardian Angel had pushed a book onto the floor in my presence.

Not one to be frightened of the Supernatural or the Unexplained, I headed over to the newly launched book. I am the sort of person who, if I was cast in a horror movie, I am the one who investigates the basement, alone, without a torch, you know, that sort of person.

I can almost hear people around me shouting 'Don't do it, step away from the book...' but no, I headed over to the book only to see the giant title glaring up at me 'Hand of God' (1996) A Journey from Death to Life, by the abortion doctor who changed his mind. I felt there was anger and determination behind bringing this message to me, I felt there was an energy reminding me that there is an intelligence which is aware of all injustice.

I was in an extremely unjust situation at the time and there wasn't a lot I could do to get out of it. I felt I had been given the message from Spirit that there is a higher authority 'in charge' even though I had no evidence of it at the time. The situation didn't end well, and in the short time there was drama and trauma, but in the long term it worked out for the best. Even with the upset and drama.

I didn't feel I needed to open the book for any other words than the title, it was enough for me on that day, and I still remember the experience to this day. It is one of those synchronistic events, which have a profound effect on the person who is being affected. This happened in the late 90s, it is now 2017. Still memorable for me.

Sometimes we are guided or drawn to randomly open a book in a charity shop or a book shop only to find the exact words we need to hear at that time. Sometimes books fall open at the exact spot we are looking for.

Funeral Balloons Story

Funerals are often gatherings where coincidental and weird events happen. One funeral I went to, everyone let go of pink balloons into the air as a final farewell only for the balloons to get trapped in the nearest tree!

Everyone had a good laugh, which was also a reminder of the person who had passed, it would have been something which he would have had a good laugh at too.

The Phoenix and the Blue Shoe Story

I had a recent series of coincidences happen around a death. The passing of my son's nan. She passed away after a long illness. She had lived a long, happy, worry-free life and she knew she was going to die. When she was on her death bed, two days before she died, I went and said my goodbyes. I wished her well on her journey and I said to her, when she dies, if there is something 'more', you know, like an afterlife, for her to let us know by sending a sign of the Phoenix.

I wasn't honestly expecting to see a Phoenix anywhere because it is all so unknown isn't it? If a person doesn't believe that you should communicate with people in spirit, would they stick with that belief, once they are the people in spirit? Are you with me?

Bear with me, dear reader, buckle up for another long-winded story, if you hang in there, I promise all the threads will come together at the end. The funeral was a burial, a family service at a local Catholic church, followed by a trip to the cemetery for the burial service, followed by a celebration of life at another location.

After the church service, my son and his dad were walking together, and my son pointed out a blue shoe that was just sitting in the middle of their path. His dad decided that it must belong to his aunty, not an obvious conclusion to jump to, but as it turned out, he was right. They rescued the shoe and later in the day, his aunty mentioned that she had lost a shoe. My son and his dad were able to reunite her with the shoe. Bear with me dear reader, I promise there is a point to this story.

A little while later, my son and I went to the cinema to see the blockbuster of the summer. The film called 'NOPE', directed by Jordan Peele. During the film, in a random scene, which was a little odd, there was a blue shoe, just standing up, unsupported, by itself, in the middle of the scene. Without explanation and seemingly randomly. I nudged my son, look, a blue shoe! NOPE, he wasn't having any of it. He sees it that I am making connections where there aren't any. Which is fair enough. It wasn't until the characters in the film started chatting with each other that I noticed one of the children was called Phoenix. That was enough for me to think, yes, there it is. Those two things, the single blue shoe and the name Phoenix, connected with my son's nan and her funeral, was enough of a sign for me to enjoy and see it as a 'Hello' from the afterlife. I think it was Stuart Chase who said, 'For those who don't believe, there is not enough evidence, for those who believe, no evidence is necessary'. (**Stuart Chase**)

I take these signs as a nod from Spirit that my son's nan made it to the afterlife. Skip forward a few months and although I haven't written down every time a phoenix shows up, or the mention of a phoenix, such as in the Harry Potter adverts, I have just made a mental note. I wouldn't count them as meaningful though, not really, that would be assigning meaning where nothing out of the ordinary has happened, or unexpected, not really.

However, my son then decided to go back to working for an employer. He had been working for himself during the pandemic, but time was up, time to find something more challenging than working from home by himself. After his nan died, he decided to have a look around and see if there were any interesting jobs about. He liked the look of one, he applied, he interviewed, he got the job.

For anyone out there who is looking for a job, you will know how competitive the job market is now. The recruitment process can often be lengthy, time-consuming and lead to disappointment. Not this time, not for my son. He found the right job at the right time for him. The first day of his new job in London, at a building with the word 'Angel' in it, he was taken out for lunch in a local pub. The name of the pub? The Phoenix.

It made me smile. I am pretty sure that his nan in Spirit had a hand in prompting him to apply for that particular job.

Dear lovely reader, if you are looking for a job, ask Spirit/Source for some help to guide you to apply for the right job.

Police Cars Story

Once upon a time, are you sitting comfortably, dear reader? Well, come with me back to somewhere in the mid-2000s, 2004-2008, somewhere in there. I lived about six roads away from an old friend and one evening we had agreed to get together for a tea and a catch up. I walked round there around 5.30-6pm and we got talking. Before we knew it, it was 8.30-9pm. It was getting dark outside and my friend offered me a lift home. I refused her offer because she had been at work all day and I knew she was tired. It was a 10–15-minute walk and it wasn't actually dark out yet.

I felt confident in my ability to walk swiftly home and make it back all in one piece. I hoofed off in the direction of my home. As I was walking along, I noticed a Police car had pulled over on the side of the road, it had its flashing blue lights on. Then I noticed a large group of teenage boys, older teenagers, not quite men, not quite teenagers, those inbetweeners, in hoodies, with some of them sitting on BMX bikes.

I wondered what they had done, I could see them watching me walk towards them. I was fully confident in the Police and whatever they were doing there. As I walked nonchalantly through the group, another Police car drove up and pulled up in front of the first Police car, facing it. Two Police cars, facing each other, next to me in the road as I walked past. One of them, obviously, on the wrong side of the road.

I walked about 10-15ft to the next junction. Through the teenagers who had fallen silent as I walked through. I checked the traffic before I started crossing the fourth road on my way home. I couldn't hear any traffic, but, as is my nature to double-check I glanced back over my shoulder. There were no cars coming. There were no Police cars either.

I crossed the road as swiftly as my legs would carry me and put as much distance between me and the teenagers as I could. I glanced back a couple of times just to make sure the Police cars weren't there. They had vanished in an instant.

Clearly, dear reader, I have given this a lot of thought since it happened, and wondered where they went. I have concluded that they were never there in the first place. But I must tell you, they looked as real as the teenagers that I felt they were protecting me from.

They couldn't have driven off without me seeing them. It was seconds that I was walking towards the only junction one of the cars could have turned up. The first Police car that was on the left, facing the right way, would have had to drive around the second Police car and pulled out to pull round it to get up the road. It would have had to drive past me.

The car facing the other way would have had to have been travelling at a vast rate of knots for me not to have noticed it driving away from me. There were no Police cars.

It was mysterious and weird, and I realise that by sharing this sort of experience, it can easily make people doubt my sanity. I promise you dear reader, it happened to me. I didn't imagine it. I am as sane as can be expected at this stage of the game!

Category 9
Data

The Information Stream. It is a never-ending stream and it can come from all directions. It can show up in the form of dates, names, places, events, times or numbers. You know, the actual signs, signs in public, with words written on them. I call these suburban messages.

I find these types of coincidence the most amusing, they are the most everyday type of coincidence, but every now and then, one will show up which feels like it was meant to be, and you were in the right place at the right time to see it.

Suburban messages

I had a friend once who was suffering emotional turmoil over whether to put the process of divorce proceedings into action. She had gone so far along the divorce path and the next step was to sign some forms from which there was no return, no going back, it would lead to divorce.

This is how she felt about it, not because she couldn't change her mind, but because her husband wouldn't have forgiven her for going behind his back and asking for mediation and help with sorting out the finances.

We had a tarot reading session and my friend headed home to deal with the difficult decision between a safe home and unhappy marriage or a poverty-stricken future, homelessness and single parenthood.

I strolled to my local supermarket to buy a pint of milk. On my way back there was a leaflet which had been dropped on the ground with DIVORCE written in giant white letters on a purple background. It was an advert for a divorce lawyer. The coincidence did not escape me, I took a photo and sent it to my friend.

I have another friend who was talking about her job to her work colleagues, she said to them 'This job is like walking through mud'. As she left her office, she noticed a car pull in front of her with the number plate 'MUD'. It made her laugh and served as a reminder of the spookiness of the Universe that we are living in.

Dates with Destiny

A spin-off the number game. Noticing coincidental birth dates, death dates, marriages, graduations, passing driving tests, you name it, there are significant dates which we all have, and those dates and times are woven into our lives.

Often the dates will recur and so we are always aware

of that one significant date. For me, I have a few significant dates, birth dates, and the number 13, generally.

Friday 13th Story

I do love to tell the story of my driving test date. Friday 13th is considered by some to be a fateful day, or more specifically, an unlucky day and so, years ago, when you put in for your driving test and waited three weeks to have confirmation of your driving test date and time sent through the post, if you were unlucky enough to be booked on Friday 13th, chances are you would be cancelling that test and re-applying for a more auspicious date.

So, if, like me, you enjoy playing with the number 13, and you are happy to book a short notice cancellation test, one that someone else has cancelled, just before a Friday 13th, that is going to be the most likely date for your test.

It was no surprise really that I passed my driving test on Friday 13th, as did my brother, and my dad. Three of us all passed our tests on Friday 13th.

Meaningful Dates Story

The most improbable date coincidence I have heard of involves a house viewing and a town with a funny name. I went to spiritualist church regularly and I used to have a little chat with the regulars about all manner of weird and wonderful experiences. One lady had said she was thinking about moving. Her husband wanted to move closer to Norwich, but they had no idea precisely where they wanted to go.

One night, my church friend was looking on the map of Norwich and noticed a town called Little Snoring, she pointed it out to her husband and said she didn't mind where they went as long as it wasn't there. They both laughed it off.

Fast forward a few weeks and a few dozen estate agents later, having given all their search criteria to some local experts, some house viewings had been arranged. A little bungalow had come up, did they want to see it? It ticked all their boxes, their garden requirement, parking, garage, you name it, it had everything they wanted. They phoned up to book a viewing only to discover it was in the town with the funny name! They laughed, they decided to see it anyway.

The day of the viewings, the couple pulled up onto the driveway and immediately loved the property on the outside. Once inside the home, the couple had a look around all the rooms and found themselves standing in the central hallway, having a chat with the owner.

My church friend happened to glance up as she admired one of the wooden beams over the master bedroom doorway. She noticed an etching in the wood, it was a date. The owner explained, it was the date she had given birth to her son, at home, in that room. My church friend could not believe what she was seeing, the date, the day, the month and the year, was the same as their wedding anniversary. They went on to buy the house, despite the silly name of the town!

Music

Song Lyrics which have meaning for us. Often after death communication comes in the form of coincidence of hearing songs.

All creative works seem to be used by the Universe. Whether it is a line from a song, a poem, or a book, the art provokes a reaction from the individual and it is the sense of special meaning that it holds for that person which is the key.

Songs in your head can pop up in answer to a question, the words of the song have specific meaning for you at this time, this literal second in time, or on a bigger level, around a bigger question you may have been asking or as a message from spirit. Sometimes the song comes to you as a memory, a train of thought, or someone mentions the song in passing, but often it comes in the form of hearing the music being played somewhere.

Music is data, lyrical, emotive, beautiful data. Perhaps because we attach deep meaning to specific words and songs, music is often found to be at the centre of a synchronistic event, or at least a coincidence.

You know the experience, you have someone in spirit who always used to sing their favourite song, usually tunelessly and the memory of them singing brings a smile to your face. Just as you are thinking of your loved one, their song comes on the radio.

Straight after a conversation about your loved one, you jump in your car, turn the radio on, and voila, the song comes on again. You drive home, once indoors, you turn the telly on, only to hear the same song as a backing track to a show. Right at that precise moment. You have a feeling you are being contacted, you love the experience, it may bring up feelings for you about your loved one, but know, that these words which are coming to you are ways for your loved one to communicate with you from Spirit.

For me, that song is 'Dancing Queen., by Abba. What a great song. It is a classic, admittedly, and I have heard it on two separate television programmes this week. I heard it on Michael McIntyre's new show on a

Saturday night, on BBC. Michael McIntyre secretly teamed up with a lady who let him into her home at 3 am to surprise her husband! Michael woke him up at 3 am by strolling into his bedroom with a television crew and delivering a quiz. One of the questions was a person dressed up in a white lycra catsuit, singing a song which the poor unsuspecting husband had to identify. The song was 'Dancing Queen', by Abba.

Over on the other main channel, ITV, Ant and Dec, the pair of tv presenters who have been a staple of British Television since they were teenagers, they are now in their forties, were presenting 'I'm a Celebrity, Get Me Out Of Here', a reality tv show where a dozen celebrities of varying degrees of fame are thrown into a jungle camp environment and forced to play games in order to win meals and treats.

This week, the celebrities were put into an old car, one celeb had headphones with music playing in, whilst having insects in their mouth they had to hum the tune. The Celeb's teammate had to guess the tune. Again, the song was 'Dancing Queen', by Abba.

This is a coincidence. It is. Does it have any specific meaning? Well, for me, the song does have a deeper meaning. When I was aged 10, my 15-year-old brother committed suicide. He climbed up an electricity pylon and jumped off. He left a note. There was no doubt. He wanted his life to be over. Naturally, this destroyed my mum, my other brother was 13 at the time and he was devastated, as was I.

Fortunately for me, I miraculously had a love of reading, which saved me, firstly, by allowing me to have fantasy worlds in which to escape, and secondly by offering self-help in the form of wise words from people who had taken the time to share their knowledge and experience. I am ever grateful to every author who has managed to complete a book which is able to help people who have no other source of support.

I digress, my Mum suffered the loss in such a deep way that 40 years later, I can say with hindsight, that she pretty much stopped functioning for a while. There was no support in Wickford, Essex in the 1970s. There were a lot of pointing fingers as she used alcohol to soothe the pain, how she managed to carry on, as a single parent of two grieving youngsters, I will never know. But she did, she went on to quit alcohol, qualify as a hypnotherapist and write a book of short stories (Sun Signs in Love by Unice McGregor).

Anyway, back to the 70s, it had been a couple of years, in a home filled with loss and no laughter. We had been living in a bungalow when my brother killed himself. It was April in the mid-seventies. Ten days before Christmas, the Council gave us Notice that the bungalow we were renting was being knocked down to make way for a main road to ease traffic congestion in Wickford.

We were moved into a rented house in Swan Lane. It was years of misery, tears, cold, poverty and loss. My surviving brother grew up rapidly and moved out of the house and went to stay with the family of a friend he was at school with.

Something shifted for my Mum, I think it began to dawn on her that life carries on. Her world may have come to an end, but I was still there, growing up in front of her. I came home from school one day, instead of the usual silence and cold, my mum was standing next to a newly purchased record player (a big deal in the seventies in a poverty-stricken household).

She was waiting for me to come home from school, waiting with the record lined up to play 'Dancing Queen., by Abba.

We danced and laughed and played the record on repeat. It was the start of a long, painful journey towards recovery, and it began with a song for which I will be forever grateful.

When songs have meaning, either the songs you hear exactly match the events you have going on in your life or the thoughts you are thinking at that moment.

When you have a special song with someone, that reminds you of that person, you hear the song and then that person contacts you or bumps into you. Once you have learned to harness the synchronicity in your life, you will notice the song and you will not even be surprised when you see the person. Better yet, you will pick up the phone and call them first.

Tamasin F. Blake

I'd Like to Teach the World to Sing Story

I could just give you the facts, dear reader, but where would be the fun in that? Recounting my coincidental stories with a little back story, does bring life to the story. The facts are fun, the actual coincidence is the fact, but by giving you a bigger picture helps me to share the meaning the coincidence held for me at the time.

Some time around 2010 I was fortunate enough to be living in Leigh on Sea in Essex, which, according to a recent survey, is The Happiest Place to Live in the United Kingdom.

I was making the best of my situation as a single parent on a low income, working part-time and permanently trying to figure out how to increase my income and so improve the lifestyle for myself and my son.

I kept up my habit of attending church as often as I could. Usually once a week on a Wednesday afternoon. Not every week, but whenever I was free. My church of choice is a spiritualist church. I love the address given by the mediums, usually as an opener to the service. There is also a demonstration by the medium, and the messages are often uplifting, heartfelt and touching for the person on the receiving end. I love to hear all the messages, whether they are for myself or for other people.

I am also very fortunate to have been blessed with the ability to see psychic activity around mediums as they are working on the platform. I see this in the form of coloured cloud/light up on the podium with them. I have seen mediums surrounded in green light, like the old Ready Brek advert where a family eat breakfast cereal, and they go out for their working day or school day glowing with the warm orange body-shaped light which keeps them warm as they walk into the cold light of day.

I have seen a medium share her podium with a giant cloud of purple light, and I have watched as it appeared to feed into her mind through a skull cap sized white circle of light on the side of head. She offered amazing messages to people in the congregation. The little church which I am referring to is in Leigh on Sea, St. Cecilia's in Lord Roberts Avenue. (Another coincidental Robert, for me, the name of my brother in Spirit). I am sure most people who attend church on a regular basis, do so because they feel they have a special connection, and their church holds a special place in their heart. But, for St Cecilia's, everyone who attends the church does say there is a special feel to this church. It is a small haven, a peaceful, healing vibration emanates through the altar, the podium, the carpets, the curtains, and the red-covered chairs, most of them with little brass plaques on the back with names of people who have passed over, regular visitors to the church who have prayed, meditated and communicated with spirit from within the safety of St Cecilia's walls.

One Wednesday afternoon, I struck up conversation with a lady sitting behind me. The nature of this small church is that just before the service, most of the congregation will have a little chat and join together in a little socialisation, we are all aware that some of us are lonelier than others, some of us aren't at all lonely, but we all know our role.

To join in and chat with everyone, it is very British, no-one has to put their hand up and say, 'I'm feeling lonely today', everyone has someone to chat with if they need it. So, this week, less than a dozen people were in the congregation and one of them was changing the CDs at the back of the room. Half a dozen people were given messages from a lovely medium, not me though, not this time. I wasn't given a message, but I loved listening to people responding to the medium and I enjoyed the songs.

Another reason I enjoyed going along for a Wednesday service, I found it fun and singing in a group helped me to feel better. I felt as though my spiritual batteries had been recharged, until the next time, or the next message, or the next meaningful coincidence.

We sang 'I'd like to teach the world to sing' by the New Seekers. A lady sitting in the row behind me said it had been one of her dad's favourite songs. I enjoyed the service. I walked home with icy cold rain stinging my face, but I still had a warm feeling to help in the battle against the rain.

The rain always seems to come down during the late afternoon time. Ask any parent who has stood in a school playground at pick up time, day in, day out, it is almost guaranteed that at school picking up time, there will be cloud burst, almost as if on cue for everyone to have wet clothes and for the journey home to be harder than it needed to be. No sooner is everyone back home indoors, the clouds dry up! Not always, but it does happen a lot.

The next day, a clear day, I was walking into Southend-on-Sea, from Leigh, it is a couple of miles and I do enjoy noticing everything that shows up on my path. The people, the shops, the houses, the road names. I like to pay attention to as many details as I can. I was walking towards a second hand/antique shop, a curiosity shop in Westcliff.

On the path up ahead, I noticed a black disc. On the grey pavement, a few feet away from the curiosity shop. I guess someone must have dropped it, either on the way in or on the way out.

As I walked closer to it, I realised it was a vinyl disc, a record. As is my way, naturally, I had to be nosy and peek at the title of the record:

'I'd like to teach the world to sing' by the New Seekers.

What are the chances? I loved the coincidence, and I took it as a sign that Spirit had been with me as I was in Church on the Wednesday.

Remembering people in Spirit by their favourite sayings

When people are on the planet, living, breathing, having a life and living their day-to-day world, they have beliefs which they sometimes share with their loved ones. Sometimes all people can do is offer oft-repeated sayings and beliefs in answer to a loved one's problems, sayings such as:

'Keep smiling' or 'Laugh and the world laughs with you, cry and you cry alone.'

'Every cloud has a silver lining' – one of my personal favourites.

'Cross that bridge when you come to it'.

'There's always one'.

Sayings that people say to you, repeatedly. When you hear certain sayings repeatedly, there is a message within those words. I do know some people think that hearing a message three times gives it more power. For me, hearing a common saying, such as 'you can choose your friends, but you can't choose your family' is a reminder of the deeper meaning of those words. The message is for you to remember that you must love your family. A pre-arranged agreement between you in Spirit before you incarnated that you have karma to work out and you can only do that with forgiveness and love. Love your family, let them go, feel love for them, think healthy loving thoughts and let the karma go.

But for someone whose nan used this as her personal mantra, the person hearing it will have a different emotional effect on them. It is the meaning it has for the individual who is hearing the words.

Category 10
Numbers

We are surrounded by numbers. Some days there are more numbers than others, granted, but we are all exposed to numbers on a daily basis. For most of us there is a house number, a flat number, or a room number. For even more of us, there are telephone numbers, codes we use as employees, bus routes we take, numbers for the roads we travel on. Everywhere you look, there are usually numbers. The television set you watch, usually has a model number, the laptop you type on, the computer screen you look at. Numbers. Car park spaces are numbered, lanes for queuing, numbered, train station platforms, airport terminals and gates, they all have numbers.

It can be interesting to write down whichever numbers show up for you, either daily, weekly, monthly or if your memory is good enough, at the end of each year. The reason I try and do this is because I know that at some stage, one of the numbers will have a deep significance and I will be able to use my diary to track back, to see where I was, emotionally, mentally, physically, financially and spiritually, at the time.

As Terence McKenna pointed out, there are schizophrenics who think that EVERY number plate carries a message for them, EVERY overheard conversation is about them, whether it is relevant to them or not. Whether the number plate has any relevance for them at the time, or not, they make the number plate fit.

A quick mention of Nikola Tesla, the man who gave us alternating current and invented a radio controlled boat, not to mention attempting to figure out how to harness the power of the Universe to bring us wireless lighting and electricity.

This man who is hailed as one of the finest minds in the history of humanity, also talked about the 3,6,9 sequence. He wrote and thought about the trifecta of energy, frequency and vibration and declared the numbers 3,6 and 9 to be the keys of the Universe. He also had an affinity with the number 18, which is divisible by 3, 6 and 9.

Noticing Number 47 Story

Apart from keeping a journal of the coincidences I experience as I am writing this book, I am asking you to Test the Universe for yourselves. Since there is a vast amount of information available on the internet, naturally, since researching coincidences for this book, I have found information that I was unaware of previously. Such as, the random appearance of Number 47.

Apparently, this is a number which appears so frequently there is a website and a group who recognise the weirdness of this number. It has never shown up for me, never been a number with any significance. At all. Or so I thought. I decided that I would use this new number, new to me, as the number I am going to pay attention to in my world, as my own personal Test Subject. I know this is going to sound stupid, but this is literally the first time I have noticed my own mobile phone number ends in 47. I always think of the last three digits of my number which is 147. I didn't make the connection between this common number and my own phone number. There it was. Hiding in plain sight.

I also noticed a little mini car, parked on the road, near my house, with the plate P** 147. There, a sign from the Universe that I am lining up with synchronistic numbers.

The thing about numbers is that they are everywhere, it is easy to find patterns in the numbers, looking for patterns and coincidences, yes, it is easy to start believing you are reading something into something which isn't there, you are making it up, you are hoping this to have some meaning. Giving meaning where none exists is an easy thing to do, but once you have found your own numbered pathway, they are almost impossible to ignore or avoid.

Avoiding Number 137 Story

I decided I am going to play the avoid game while I am writing this book. I am going to avoid the number 137, a number which has not had any significance for me, as far as I am aware, and yet there are many people who feel this number is an enigma, and the weirdest number in the Universe.

Since I do love to play with the Universe and I am open to new ideas, I thought it would be interesting to see what shows up! It occurred to me to just check which day of the year is the 137th day...well, it has no significance for me. I checked the www.epochconverter.com which has all manner of days of the year.

Number of the day, numbers to go until the end of the year, numbers for your heart's delight. I checked every which way, and the 137 showed no coincidence, for me, any which way I checked it. This is the enigma of 137.

As I was editing this portion of the book, one of my friends, who I have known for over 25 years, sent me a Facebook message asking for my postcode so she can send me a Christmas card. I grabbed my address book to check where I was sending her card. Her house number? 137.

There isn't really a lot of data available nor has any serious research been done into the patterns of different numbers for different people. I can only speak from my experience of speaking with people over a forty-year period, a natural interest in people's life experiences and enjoying chats about the esoteric, paranormal, coincidences and generally unexplained events that happen to people.

I have found that birth dates tend to crop up for people as lucky numbers. It is a mystery as to why certain numbers show up for people, it could be that people only notice numbers which have meaning for them, the same way our human brain is created/designed to recognise patterns of faces, so show us an ink blot or a shadow on Mars and we are likely to be able to distinguish a pattern of a face, even when there is no face there.

There is no way of knowing if the number shows up because the person is attaching meaning to that number, so they attract more of that number. Even that as a phenomenon is a stretch to believe, it really is a thing.

Noticing Multiple Numbers

I have a few coincidental stories around numbers. I do love to uncover the patterns, and I find they are fairly easy to spot.

I started paying attention to recurring numbers when

they began showing up in triplicate. 111 to be precise. It seemed to show up everywhere, at the time, everywhere I went, the number 111 would show up. Or I would notice it. It was probably always there, and I never paid it any mind. (Editing this book in May 2023, I went swimming 520m, I tapped into my health app the length of time it took me and my little app calculates how many calories I used up. Do I need to tell you, dear reader, how many calories the app thinks I used up? That's right, 111).

The number 11:11 regularly showed up on clocks. I feel the numbers are like a Universal Clock, 11:11 especially, is time to wake up. Wake up to your spiritual nature. A prod from the Universe to remember your spiritual nature which brought you here. Prior to my noticing the 11:11 number showing up, I had noticed 666, quite often. The 666 had played a role in grabbing my attention. I was born in 1966 and my bank account from the age of 18 also ended in a triple 666.

After about a year of what felt like being stalked by triple 111, the number 333 started showing up, also 12:12 and 13:13 had a turn, the numbers 321, 444, 555, 666, 777, 888 and 999. My journey through seeing these numbers regularly did take about a year for each set of numbers, but not always consecutively.

I do remember the year of 888. I had two mobile phone sim cards sent through the post from Virgin Media, unsolicited, unexpected and frankly unwanted, until I noticed the numbers both ended in triple eight. I had a wonderful year with that 'lucky' phone number. I thoroughly enjoyed it.

I particularly enjoyed the year of 444, which is associated with Guardian Angels. One day I decided to take a walk out into my local neighbourhood, asking my Guides to prompt me in whichever direction I needed to go. I went for a stroll into Southend-on-Sea town centre, across a busy High Street, through a cemetery and found myself in the middle of a car park. I thought to myself, communicating with my guides 'What did you want me to see here?'

I was about to turn round and walk straight home when I was prompted to explore a little further, looking behind me I noticed a Rossi ice-cream van parked sideways on to me, so I couldn't see the number plate. walked right into the closed depot, around the front of the ice-cream van. The number plate was 444. I took a photo, thanked the Universe and my Angels. I shared the photo to Facebook and went home feeling cloaked in the warmth of spirit, knowing that we are accompanied by our Guardian Angels at every step.

As I was working on the number 444, writing this book, I had reason to send off for a new bank card. The bank dutifully sending a new chip and pin code for me to learn and consequently dispose of. I was loathe to dispose of the number, which had three fours in it, but for security purposes, naturally, I had to change it, but not before thanking the Universe for the lovely little coincidental number which made me happy.

Number 251 Story

I used to have the number 251 show up repeatedly, for years. I travelled on the number 251 bus from Wickford in Essex to Southend-on-Sea, also in Essex, when I moved to Southend-on-Sea, I moved to a house number 251. (As I write my journal, alongside this book, I am reminded that I was given £2.51 change in a shop today).

Even more fun is when the numbers show up unexpectedly and in such a way that it cannot just be coincidence, the feeling of such an experience brings a mystical wonder which touches your heart and helps you to feel that you are being watched over and helped. A feeling of numinosity.

Number 107 Story

The number 107 also spent some time in my world, and my son's world. We lived in a flat number 107a Hildaville Drive, in Westcliff, which was once the home of Stand-Up Comic, Lee Evans. The comedian from Essex had once delivered a sketch about his time living in the flat, describing how both his neighbours lived in bungalows, flat 107a, was nestled between two bungalows and there were no other bungalows in the street. The flat my son and I lived in, matched the description given by Lee Evans during one of his shows. I heard this information from a woman who just happened to be walking past my front door, carrying a large standard lamp, as I was walking up the path. I joked 'Travelling light?', as is my way, you know, because I do think I am funny. Fortunately, the lady laughed, putting her lamp on the pavement, she stopped to share her Lee Evans story with me.

During my son's time between studying, my son had the opportunity of a holiday of a lifetime in Thailand. A school friend's family had all booked a Villa in Thailand, a family of teachers, mum was a teacher, dad was a teacher, their eldest daughter and her husband were teachers, and my son was at Uni the same time their younger daughter was at Uni. They had space in their villa for my son to join them and they invited my son to join them on their family holiday, which was so generous of them and for those generous people I will be forever grateful. As a single parent on a low income, travel to Thailand with my son was an impossibility for me. They were flying out to Thailand on the first day of the school holiday, putting the airfare at over £1000 at the time. If they travelled the day before, there were flights going for £500.

My son set to the Internet, a quick google search to find matching flights so he could join them on their journey, a journey from London to Thailand in the safety of a family we had known for years, wonderful. Unfortunately, or fortunately, depending on which way you look at saving £500, there were no seats available on their flights. Mainly due to short notice, but also due to the flight date being the first day of the school holidays. My son, being an optimistic, 'no problem' type, decided he would take a flight a day earlier and wait on the beach for his friend and her family to arrive. Over my dead body. I felt I needed to insist that he find at least some form of accommodation for the night, perhaps a student hostel, shared room situation.

My son gave in and booked a room for £15.00 a night in a place that had my name in it, 'Tam...' something. I liked that idea. It comforted me that this place existed, and he was at least going to be inside at night. I wondered how bad it could be for £15.00 a night? What I didn't realise is that you could book a room in Thailand for 50p a night.

He arrived in Thailand and took a cab to the address. The cab dropped my son off to his £15.00 a night room, which turned out to be his own private villa in the centre of a lake with an all you can eat fresh buffet for breakfast. He sent me a photo of the villa, to put my mind at rest, and also because he knew I enjoyed the coincidence of the numbers. We were living in flat 107A and the Villa Number was A107. I thanked the Universe and knew he was being helped by Spirit/God/The Universe, a higher intelligence.

Number 23 Story

Speaking of random numbers which seem to show up with alarming regularity, the number 23 seems particularly guilty. So guilty, in fact, it has been featured in a Jim Carrey movie. (The Number 23).

If you really want your mind to be spun a little more, please see my later chapter about weird and wonderful things, including the Mandela Effect. I do believe Jim Carrey has not always been called Jim Carrey, he used to be known as Jim Carey. But, as you will discover as you read the Mandela chapter, this is a memory or a residue from another dimension, or experience of an alternate reality. A quantum leap of faith, if you will, that we are living not in a Universe but in a multi-verse. More on that later.

007 story

In 1990, a 15-year-old school student called James Bond sat his High School GCSE exam at Argoed, Flintshire, North Wales. The exam paper reference number was 007.

Chapter III
Anti-Synchronicity

"Anything that can go wrong, will go wrong"

Edward A. Murphy Jr.

Murphy's Law is a humorous reminder that despite our best efforts, unexpected problems, setbacks, or errors can occur in various situations. The term originated from Edward A. Murphy Jr., an American aerospace engineer, during the late 1940s. It was named after him when he mentioned it in reference to a failed experiment where the wiring was incorrectly installed.

There are so many sayings that people use to denote the awfulness of it all! There is no shortage of examples, and I am sure, dear reader, that you have had the experience where a stream of negative statements has just tripped off your tongue. I am sure you can think of some, even as you are reading this, sayings like:

It never rains but it pours.

Hope for the best but prepare for the worst.

Just my luck

Sounds about right.

Don't count your chickens before they hatch.

Don't speak too soon.

I have a black cloud hanging over me.

Bad luck follows me like a cloud.

Things always turn out bad for me.

I always make the wrong decisions.

The examples of things that can go wrong are also seemingly never-ending, you know the sort of things that happen:

You have missed the last bus and you need to call someone to pick you up, your phone is on the last 1% and you use it to call the wrong person. You waste your last little bit of battery apologizing to someone who you hadn't even meant to call. Or the washing machine breaks down just when you have a job interview to attend to and your best shirt needs cleaning.

The strange thing I have noticed about these anti-synchronistic events is that they seem to happen in clusters.

It isn't simply your phone running out of battery, it is your phone running out of battery at the worst possible moment. These are the stories that a lot of people are in the habit of telling. Engaging a willing audience and getting them to share in the awfulness of it all.

When you first start playing with the Universe and examining where synchronicity shows up in your world, see if you find it easier to spot a meaningful coincidence which led to fortuitous circumstances or one where it led to an unfortunate sequence of events.

As you practice paying attention to the events in your own personal world, it does become easier to live in the moment and notice the coincidences at the time. Most people live through their lives, they live some experiences and then they look back over the experience, afterwards. Living life by looking in the rearview mirror is a good way to start.

It has been my experience that people who are in the habit of noticing what has gone wrong with their lives, are also highly emotive about whatever it is that went wrong, like the traffic, the delays, the missed plane, usually finding fault with the airline or whoever they feel has caused the disaster.

The next step is to get just as excited about the things that worked, the things that went right, when it all worked out for you.

When people look back over disaster which has befallen them in a way which doesn't really have any long-term consequences, they rarely analyse the situation like a forensic analyst would. Generally, it is only when the situation has long term consequences, such as, a person dying, or suffering from a life-changing accident, people stop to check a) who was to blame for this or b) could I have done anything different.

How many times have people had to be talked down from blaming themselves for everything? I experienced a burglary once, I thought I was burgled because I didn't put the extra padlock on the side gate when I was house sitting (I was convinced it was my fault). It wasn't my fault, it was the burglar who broke in whose fault it was, not to mention a distinct lack of burglar alarm. Victims blame themselves for being in the wrong place at the wrong time.

The little old lady who blames herself for being mugged 'I shouldn't have been carrying a brightly coloured handbag'. No, this wasn't her fault. It was the fault of the mugger.

But these coincidences do exist. The coincidence of a mugger, an opportune mugger, having his attention drawn to the brightly coloured bag of an old lady who was also aware that she had valuable items in her bag. Both having their attention drawn to the precious object, bang, synchronicity struck.

Not in a good way. In this instance, the lady was pushed over, she broke her hip, went to hospital and never recovered from the experience. She died not long after. Was it the fault of the mugger? Her family thought so. Was it meant to happen to orchestrate the end of her life? No-one knows.

How was anyone meant to know that this string of events was going to lead to a death? It does happen, it happens every day, but when a set of events leads to a death there tends to be a more critical analysis of how the events happened. After the event.

When it all goes wrong. What does it mean? The obstructions, the changes of plan, the misunderstandings, the communication which doesn't work, none of it happens by accident.

Getting lost, being lost, missing a plane, train or automobile. Being in disharmony with people around you. Plans going awry, double-booked tables, losing travel tickets, passports, visas, wallets, keys, phones.

Sometimes the diversion thrown on your path by the Universe is for your own good. Not always, but often the subtle energies are part of the programme. You know, like in a computer game, there is something else to 'mine' here for information that will be useful or helpful to you, or your timing is off and this delay will re-calibrate your time and place to put you exactly where you need to be.

What does it mean? Well, it is easy to look back and see what you should have done. For me, I would never ignore an obstruction or an obstacle. I always take the path of the least resistance. Things which tend to happen on an anti-synchronicity day seem to happen in clusters, or more specifically, in threes.

Things like, the dog does his business in the hall, or you tread in dog mess, a toilet won't flush, all manner of weird unpleasant sewage-like smells emanate in your vicinity, both inside and outside of the house and as you leave for work you lock yourself out. You know the sort of thing.

Stubbing your toes, hurting your own body. A sure sign you are beside yourself. Ignore yourself at your peril. Things like catching your clothes, ruining clothes, catching tights, breaking heels on shoes, buttons falling off clothes, traffic jams, unpleasantness from other people, snide remarks from other people, unexpected expenses or bills, uneasy gut feelings, fear, terror, arguments with your loved ones, getting sick, headaches, losing possessions, breaking objects. The list goes on.

Pre-Employment Warning Signs Story

One day, a long, long time ago, for me personally, measured by three house moves, it does seem a lot longer ago that it probably actually was! C.2009 when the Tory Government were just bringing in the Bedroom Tax legislation.

I was desperately looking for a job at the time. All jobs, any jobs, everywhere in Essex. It was a particularly difficult time for me. I had no support from anywhere, no vehicle, no savings, no funding from anywhere. I was working part-time as an Avon Rep, and I had a part-time job in the local co-op retail store.

Working as an Avon Rep meant going out in all weathers selling cosmetics. Working evenings and weekends, to catch people at home.

So when I saw a job advert asking for an Assistant Manager of a charity shop a few train stops away (I was living in Westcliff at the time). Four days a week, part-time assisting a Manager with 30 volunteers running the place. It sounded ideal. More responsibility than I had ever been used to and which I didn't know if I was ready for, but I felt I didn't have a choice but at least to try and improve my financial situation. The pay was less than £8,000 a year.

The day of the interview arrived, and the weather was lousy, it was cold, raining, with a bitter wind. I heard on the radio that there had been a death on the train track that I was due to travel on. First thing in the morning someone had jumped off a bridge in front of a train between Pitsea and Basildon.

It is an extremely sad event when anyone takes their own life, to choose to end your life so violently, knowing you are leaving everyone who cares for you, behind, grieving and lost with no answers as to why you did it, is a very cruel ending. Not to mention the effect it would have on the train driver. It is one of the most horrific ways to commit suicide. I cannot even imagine what a person must be going through to think that throwing themselves in front of a train is the solution.

From experience, I do know it takes a while for the trains to resume their normal service after a death on the tracks. It was early in the morning and I hoped the track would be cleared by the time I needed to catch the 2.30 pm train. Sitting on the train on my way to the interview which was due at 3 pm. There was a bang on the train and I knew something had hit the train, my mind briefly flashed on the idea that it could be an abandoned trolley on the track. But sadly, no, it was another suicide, on the same track, from the same bridge as earlier in the day.

I was sat with my fellow commuters on a stalled train which was promptly declared a crime scene. Men in white haznat suits came walking up the track in their wellies. We had a chat, us half a dozen commuters. We had quite a while to get to know each other. I called my prospective boss and explained the situation, he could hang on until 4 but no longer. We didn't escape the train until well after 4 pm, with darkness drawing in, we were all helped as we climbed off the train, onto the track, we were guided in the dark, led single file 100 yards along the side of the track, against wind and rain, alongside my fellow depressed commuters, down some hidden steps and we were led to a replacement bus service.

The bus driver promptly got lost on the way back to the train station. One wrong turn was all it took, I eventually made it home way after 6 pm.

I should have seen those events as Emergency Red Flags from the Universe. DO NOT TAKE THIS JOB. DO NOT GO IN THIS DIRECTION. YOU ARE GOING THE WRONG WAY.

But, like I say, my physical, financial and material needs were pressing and I didn't feel I had any option. I re-interviewed later, secured the job and started work. In good faith. I started work and the boss promptly went off sick. Other staff members leaving, and volunteers were a high turnover workforce. I was left to manage a massive charity shop, and organise 30 volunteers, full time for wages which still didn't leave me with a disposable income, because of the exorbitant rent and bedroom tax.

It was one of the worst stretches of my life. It did feel like a prison sentence that I couldn't easily find a way out of. If only I had paid attention to the Universe, practically shouting at me. I could have avoided what turned out to be an extremely stressful, unpleasant and unfair situation.

By way of an update, I have learnt from this experience. Now, whenever I have an interview, I remain in a highly vigilant state and if ever there is the slightest hint of anything not right, I walk away. Sooner, rather than later.

Chapter IV

Synchronicity Journal as I was writing this book

Synchronicities which happened as I was writing this book. The theory of the Law of Attraction and the latest belief from physicists is that whatever you focus on will get bigger. It will become more, whatever it is, whether you are focusing on lack and what you don't have and what you wish you did have, or whether you are appreciating the amazing gifts the Universe is bestowing upon you on a daily basis, fresh air, water, space to move, so, naturally, writing this book and using my mind to consider synchronicity and coincidence, the coincidences increase.

I don't believe there is any such thing as an ordinary coincidence, but there are some recurrent events which happen more often than the strange, inexplicable synchronicities we all love to be astounded by.

By way of example, I have kept a record of the coincidences which have shown up for me as I was writing this book.

I always think it is a good idea to keep a diary of whatever events show up in your world. Whether events went according to plan, was there a rescue? Did someone change some part of your plan or day, which changed the way your day panned out? Notice who you met up with as result of the different path you found yourself on.

Write down what would have happened or what wouldn't have happened if the connecting links had failed or if something else had happened. Write it down if nothing out of the ordinary happened. The more you pay attention to the ordinary, the more likely it is to become extraordinary.

Nothing happens out of the blue. Or as Esther Hicks calls it 'out of the oblivious'. You may have only just noticed it, it may have only just come to our attention, but there will have been a build-up to which we may have been blind.

Who did you bump into this week. People you know? No-one you know? Even if you didn't meet anyone you know, who did you have reason to speak with? Did you see someone walking a dog, were they smiling? Did the dog pay you any attention?

Whatever you are noticing around you, is what you have lined up with, so if you see strange events around you, like, people shouting at traffic wardens or people arguing, that is a reflection for you to know that the vibrational electric-magnetic field which is pulsing from your body, is attracting that. Whether you feel that is wanted or unwanted, personally I would find that unwanted as I prefer peace and harmony amongst people.

The Universe talks back to us, all the time, using words, typed, written, drawn, spoken, overheard snippets of conversation, song lyrics, all manner of communication comes to us if we have the ears to hear it.

Messages from the Universe can come directly in the form of words written on book Titles, or advertising slogans, printed leaflets, tickets, all forms of copywriting which the supermarket is full of.

Social media is an amazing source of possible synchronicities, not least because the computer is already deliberately working in the background to link up people with products, events and stories they may have interest in.

Pay attention to what shows up on your twitter, Facebook, snapchat, all forms of meetings, albeit not IRL, but in a Virtual IRL. If you can see the symbolism and attach meanings to the pictures, words, names and numbers which show up, the internet has to be the largest source of information for you to work with.

Ask for something specific in advance, choose a colour – Pink/Blue/Red, choose an object – Glass/Feather. Wait for it to show up. Be mindful, give thanks to the Universe. Feel expectant, and ready to receive.

The importance of colours which show up in your world are an added level of 'evidence' for the synchronicity and exactness of the Universe to be able to prove to you that whatever you have lined up with, mastered, conjured, attracted into your life experience, however you want to feel about material objects showing up.

Choose something as complicated or as plain as you want. Ask for purple glass with yellow dots if you feel like it, if you have an understanding that the Universe is responding to your inner emotional states, which are dependent on your mental states, then you know that you can believe you will see purple glass with yellow dots and voila, it will show up. Somewhere, some way, in your world. This is playing with the Universe. It is fun, and it may feel like a coincidence that had nothing to do with you! It has everything to do with you, your Higher Self, your helpers in Spirit, your Guardian Angels, your Spirit Guide, your loved ones who may have passed over. The Universe is responding to your every thought and feeling.

The Universe is like a matrix, some people argue that it is a matrix, Elon Musk, is of the view that we are probably not even living in base reality. Meaning that we are the creation of a higher intelligence, who in turn was created by someone/something else.

This proposition means there is a lot to learn, there are many truths out there which we have yet to uncover, discover or perhaps create. As Esther Hicks, and now in Spirit, Jerry Hicks have often stated: 'You create your own reality'.

I have 'assigned meaning' to events which I have noticed keep happening for me, to me, around me, but I do feel that I am being acknowledged by my higher self whenever one of the coincidences occurs.

It is such a personal thing for each individual, this is what I am asking you to discover, what are the events that happen in your life to which you can give meaning to? We all have such different lives and so many different events happen for each of us. I can only share the ones which I have experienced.

Feel free to write your own list of symbols, meanings, and events, by ascribing your own meaning to them, you are making a commitment to your higher self that when you see x, y or z, this is what it means. It may mean keep going, it may mean stop what you are doing. The choice of meaning is up to you. Which is very exciting. I often hear people asking for a sign, and then they get the sign, something happens which they want to interpret, but they haven't ascribed any specific meaning to the event and so they have no idea what the meaning is!

For me, if something happens which is unexpected and I have no pre-conceived idea of the meaning, then I would meditate on the situation around which I have a question and feel the way to what I would want the message to mean. I would ask my own inner self for an explanation of the event.

Middle of April 2017: Also, to show you, dear reader,

evidence the Universe has given to me as proof of what I believe. I believe in Spirit, I believe there is a greater intelligence which surrounds us all the time, aware of us, helping us, sometimes nudging us and we all have our own relationship with our own helpers or Angels or Spirit Guides or our Higher Self, whatever you want to call it.

So, the coincidences we experience will be individual to us, here are a few examples of the sort of coincidences which showed up for me.

My brother in Spirit is called **Robert**, but I have been given the message from mediums on the platform at various churches, that he is now known as **Bob**. He was never called Bob on the earthplane, he went through a period of being called Rob or Robbie, but as a family we called him Robert.

In recent years the name Bob has come up with increasing frequency. I have been promising to write this book for years and the first day I decided to take action and open a document on the computer, the synchronicities began. Again. They have always been there, it is the noticing of them and appreciating them, and acknowledging them that intensifies and increases them and, in my experience, causes them to become ever more improbable.

As I was saying, having decided to write this book, I was feeling sort of accomplished, as if, having taken steps towards writing a book is almost like saying I am working towards my final goal. This is why I have put it off, because once I have completed this final task, my ultimate goal of writing a book, a goal so precious to me that there isn't anything else in the world I want to do, then, what goal will be left?

But, I have decided that having written one book won't be the end of my creativity. I will be allowed to write more than one book, or maybe not, but completing this one goal will not stop me from having other goals, nor will it be the end of my creative desires.

So, the fear of starting my book had surfaced, I had overcome it, started the massive task of writing and I decided I deserved a rest, a treat, a self-claimed pat on the back. Even though I hadn't put many words to paper, the act of overcoming the fear was what I was congratulating myself for.

I lay on the couch, had a search for a film that I knew I loved and was like bubblegum for the mind. At least that is what I thought I was doing when I chose Pirates of the Caribbean with Johnny Depp as Captain Jack Sparrow. The thing furthest from my mind was synchronicity or coincidence, or the name Bob. There is no Bob in Pirates of the Caribbean, or is there?

There I was, minding my own business, fully relaxing and mindlessly enjoying the fun of Captain Jack and his mates arguing over pieces of gold in a secret cave. Then came the scene where Jack is wielding his sword over the gold and holding court in the drunken pirate way that he does and lo and behold he uses the phrase

'Robert's your Uncle and Fanny's your Aunt'

Which struck me as such an unusual combination of words and the name Robert.

The phrase is usually 'Bob's your Uncle and Fanny's your Aunt'. I found this such an incredible coincidence. I have a son, who of course, would have had an uncle called Robert or Bob. It really wasn't a phrase I ever remember hearing in Pirates.

So, there it was. The coincidence for the day. Was it because somewhere in the back of my subconscious, I was aware that this is the phrase Johnny Depp had used, but I had never noticed before? Was it Spirit directing me to choose that film? Spirit? My Higher Self? What or whoever was the cause of it, the event happened. I had the synchronicity which had deep meaning for me personally, while I was writing this book.

Following this coincidence, I wrote it down, I kept a journal. I remembered.

10th April 2017: I had a tarot reading session with an old friend who had someone in Spirit called **Jackie**. It was an impromptu reading, my friend was in need and I had cards. Although, a bit deeper, I didn't have the cards, I had left them with her some time ago and I had reminded her this week. Unbeknownst to me, she was at rock bottom and was feeling as though she didn't know which way to turn. She wondered if I knew that is how she was feeling, was I psychic enough to be aware of her low state? No. But I am psychic enough to act on thoughts which come to me.

The idea of tracking down a set of cards I had left with her had come to me, as clear as day, a few times, and it was on the third 'prompt' that I contacted her. I use the word prompt because I can only imagine the thought came from a higher intelligence. What that is I have no idea. I can't say for sure it was from Spirit, my higher self, her higher self communicating with mine, her Guardian Angel, or the woman in spirit called Jackie? I have no idea. What I do know is that I have learnt not to ignore it. I don't just think a thought, I take action, which is what I did.

So, after seeing my friend, she went off and I sat down to watch a documentary. I chose Fear of 13, an amazing documentary/film acted out by the guy who is the subject of the documentary.

SPOILER ALERT: he went to prison for something he didn't do, lied about someone else, got himself in deeper and deeper and found himself in need of help. He found help in two forms, one, a prison officer gave him some books which he found hard to read. Instead of thinking 'I can't read that' and giving up, he chose to teach himself the words. Using a dictionary to look words up and he would make up sentences using the unknown word.

One word he uses to explain what he meant was **triskaidekaphobia**

(extreme superstition regarding the number thirteen).

Triskaidekaphobia is widespread and many people consider the number 13 unlucky. This belief has various cultural and historical origins, including religious and mythological references.

For instance, in Christianity, the Last Supper is said to have had 13 attendees, including Jesus and Judas, leading to the association of the number with betrayal and misfortune. He was talking to camera and explaining how he made up the sentences, and he gave an example of using the word triskaidekaphobia, which obviously, is the title of the film. He said '**Robert has triskaidekaphobia**...'

There it was again, the use of my brother's name in a programme where I wasn't expecting to hear it.

I was disrupted halfway through watching this documentary by my local College calling me to let me know that my Counselling Diploma Certificate had arrived and it was ready for collection. I hoofed down there at the speed of light. Alright, maybe not the speed of light, but as fast as my little feet could carry me.

I wanted to collect the Diploma and use the library scanners to copy the document over to the British

Association of Counsellors and Psychotherapists in order to sit the Certificate of Proficiency.

I was under a self-imposed deadline, admittedly, it was my choice to aim for the test on 4th May, but I really needed to have the Certificate scanned as soon as possible. I flew in to the library and caught the librarians just before closing.

There are lots of scanners in the library, tables of them, at least six, possibly 20, there are a lot. The librarian has to book the scanner and allot an hour to your library ticket, so I didn't have a choice in the number of the scanner I was allotted.

'Upstairs, first on the left...'

I started up the stairs before the librarian had ended her sentence. The scanners show on the computer screens, a big message:

'This computer is available for the next 60 minutes...or, this computer is booked for library ticket no: 000980997707 ' whatever the number is.

I knew my library number, I didn't need to know the scanner number. Logging on to the computer station, waiting for the scanner to load, I looked above my head only to see the **Number 13** on the scanner.

It was weird. I was halfway through a film about the fear of the number 13 and voila the number 13 shows up. This is how synchronicity and coincidence increase, the more you focus on it, the more of it shows up.

I carried out the task of scanning at the library, headed home, relaxed and relieved to be able to finish watching the documentary without worrying about a deadline. The story of the accidental prisoner continued, he explained, he had met a woman, somehow, I am not sure how. This woman was instrumental in supporting him on his journey to uncover the truth of his innocence, she was extremely important to him. Her name was Jackie. The same name as the woman in Spirit whom I had been talking about earlier in the day.

There was also a doctor involved in the documentary, the same doctor who was involved in the O.J.Simpson case. His name? Dr. Blake. Which is also my name. The Blake, not the Dr. And also, my brother's sirname, Robert Blake. My brother died on 3rd April in the seventies. I passed my Counselling Diploma on 3rd April forty years later. The date is now also significant for a positive reason.

Once you start writing these coincidences down and paying attention, they come so thick and fast it can be easy to feel overwhelmed by the volume of information. However, I will persevere.

11th April 2017: I was working on the chapters for this book, and I was trying to figure out if synchronicity needed a chapter for the category of Enigma, or whether all coincidences are an enigma. Naturally, I turned to friend of all researchers, google. The top example and definition of the word Enigma used a sentence to explain the meaning, as is common with thesaurus and dictionaries. The sentence used the name Madeleine, which is a French name. The coincidence there is that when I was at school, learning French, our French teacher gave all the students a French name to use when we were in class. My French name was Madeleine. How lovely, a reward of coincidence from the Universe! Thank you, Universe. The gratitude and appreciation is the key to increasing the synchronicity. I ended up taking the Enigma Category out. I had to draw a line!

23rd April 2017: Playing the board game Articulate one Sunday, after a lovely dinner cooked by my ex-mother-in-law. My son, his cousin, their nan and myself all playing a game where we had changed the rules. You are supposed to work in teams to call out a description of a word written on a card, without using the word, your teammate has to say the word you are explaining before the sand falls through an egg-timer.

We were playing our own version, where it is a free-for-all, one person does the describing and everyone else shouts out as soon as they know the word. As we were playing the game, there was a knock on the door and the other ex-daughter-in-law arrived at the house to collect my son's cousin. The clue on the card I had to describe was 'Wendy house'. The name of the person at the door? Wendy. I loved the coincidence. It is fun, the Universe does love to play.

25th April 2017: I started putting videos on Youtube, a fun thing to do, having a little chat about synchronicity. My first comment, which was very exciting to me, in itself, someone not only watched my video, but they commented! Admittedly, they commented about a book they had written, but it was the name of the book which thrilled me. Quantum Bob!

26th April 2017: An estate agent called me about a job, am I interested in interviewing? Of course I am. His name? Robert. Naturally.

27th April 2017: A recruitment consultant called me. Randomly. Turns out we share an exact birthday. Not just the day, but also the year. He was more surprised than I was, I could only apologise it is my fault, I am writing a book about coincidence.

Well, I have been on the planet for 50 years. Five decades. In that time, I have been aware of sharing a birthday with a couple of celebrities. I have never met either of these people. Although, I was in the audience of the Trisha show once and her usual angst-ridden guest was replaced by someone who thought he was a gnome and a look-a-like of a celebrity I share a birthday with. So there is that.

I had a young neighbour when I was in my thirties whose mum's birthday was on the same day as mine. I think she was the first person I had ever actually met who shared my birthday. When I was in my forties I 'met' a lady online via Deepak Chopra's 'Intent' website. We became really firm internet friends, both having a love of angels and talk radio and Deepak Chopra, only to discover that we are birthday sisters.

So, roughly every ten years I hear about or meet someone who shares my birthday. It doesn't happen often. But here we are, in the middle of coincidence ridden city and it happens again. I shouldn't be shocked. #stillshocked #shockednotshocked.

27th April 2017: The internet is an amazing source of data to find coincidences, and perhaps the search engine on Facebook is written to match up dates and names. However, when I googled my name, just to see if there is anyone else with my exact name, Tamasin Blake, what came up, on 27th April was a little posting about the birthday of Cecil Day-Lewis:

April 27th is the birthday of Cecil Day-Lewis (or Day Lewis) CBE (27 April 1904 – 22 May 1972) he was an Anglo-Irish poet and the Poet Laureate of the United Kingdom from 1968 until his death in 1972. He also wrote mystery stories under the pseudonym of Nicholas Blake. He was the father of actor Daniel Day-Lewis and documentary filmmaker and television chef Tamasin Day-Lewis.

A couple of things here, the date I looked up my name brought up the birthday of Cecil Day-Lewis, on that date, clearly a Facebook algorithm. The coincidence is that his daughter has the name as me, Tamasin, and he wrote poems using the pseudonym of Blake. Which is lovely for me, to have that connection. So, as a result of this coincidence I will have a little read of his poems, which I hadn't previously been aware of.

It was also synchronistic of me to have found this information actually on his birthday. I put this down to being in tune psychically. I had a thought from...somewhere...insert your own belief about where you believe thoughts come from, I didn't ignore it. I acted on it. I took action, okay, so it wasn't dramatic, it was just a google search, but nevertheless, it led to uncovering a coincidence which I enjoyed.

28th April 2017: I listened to a Wayne Dyer talk, where he talks about waking up at the same time every day. Usually he found people waking up between 3 am and 4 am, the same time every day, but of all the people he was talking to, he asked them to put their hands up if they have this experience.

Of the people he asked, they did all wake up at that time, but they all had different times at which they woke up. Some woke at 3:21, (another common repeating number) some woke at 3.33 and various other times. Wayne shared that he woke up at 3:13. I had cause to travel on a bus later in the day. The driver had a number on his cubicle, guess the number? That's right, **313**. #notevensurprised

29th April 2017: A tarot reading client who I felt a need to tell my 13 story. My Dad was born on 13th and he was the 13th child in the family. My client said her birthday was on 13th, her friend in spirit who we had just been speaking about had died on the 13th June, 13 years ago.

4th May 2017: There was also a 'Special Day'. You know, one of those days which you remember forever because you have been working towards it for so long. Sometimes this can be a wedding, or a special birthday or a funeral. In my case, it was an Exam Day.

As a qualified Counsellor I applied for access to the British Association of Counsellors and Psychotherapists, which involved proving my proficiency in counselling, a test if you will, timed, in exam conditions. I felt that this was the pinnacle of working towards Membership of a Professional Body, so, for me, the experience was a Big Deal.

I took my spirit guides with me. I asked to be calm before I left the house. I asked for a pleasant experience. I planned on staying in the moment as much as possible, to enjoy as many details as I could. I left the house on time, it looked like rain, so I took a brolly. I walked calmly to the station, had a pleasant interaction and laugh with the guy at the ticket booth. I noticed there was a crowd queuing at a ticket barrier.

I didn't have to queue, I strolled through, the guy held the door open for me. Not a worrying thought in my mind as the train pulled in, someone else pushed the 'open door' button, I stepped in. There was a seat for me, other people were standing. There were no delays. Again, at the next ticket barrier there was a pile-up of people, mistakenly, strangely, queuing for one barrier leaving another ticket barrier entirely free, for me, to stroll through.

I was walking from Fenchurch Street to Aldgate, Aldgate East, Whitechapel, I was planning on turning right onto commercial road and The Holiday Inn, my final destination was somewhere over there. I had a mental image from google maps before I left home. I vaguely knew where I was going.

I smiled at everyone who passed me, I was on cloud nine. I enjoyed seeing the cyclists flying ahead at the traffic lights, what a sight! Twenty or thirty cyclists just going to work. It was incredible.

I used to work in London in the late eighties, early nineties, and there was hardly ever a pack of bicycles, mainly one brave soul taking his life in his hands or a professional courier type, but definitely not a pack of working people! I was impressed. I loved them. I sent them loving thoughts. I saw someone who was lost outside the Hospital, someone else helped them. I wasn't in helping mode today. I was in Special Day for Me mode.

I saw a black cat run across a beautiful manicured green lawn. I crossed over to take a photo. This is what I do when I see symbols that I believe in, ones that have meaning for me, I make a fuss, I post them on Facebook. This little black cat, I felt, was performing for me, he was beautiful against a perfect green grass. The name of his territory was called Trinity Green, which I felt was really apt for the shade of the grass.

While I was enjoying this building I also noticed a symbol on the side of another building in Aldgate, a giant feather, a giant red feather on the side of a building called St John's something, a primary school. Well, my son's granddad, in spirit, was called John. I love seeing red feathers and I love to see feathers in unexpected places. A giant feather on the side of a building, was definitely unexpected.

I walked confidently forward, wondering how far along this road I would need to walk, time was marching on, surely I should be near the road by now? As I was thinking that, I was heading towards a massive crossroads, with no road names that I recognised. Four black crows flew over my head, crowing. I didn't ignore it. I stopped walking, popped into the nearest sweet shop where two guys both agreed that my destination was in fact down the last road I had walked past. Back I went, back on the right path, heading towards the Holiday Inn, Whitechapel, I made it, nicely in time, with time to spare in fact.

I explained to the receptionist why I was there, she said I needed the 1st floor, she would release the lift for me. I walked round to the lift which had been released and had locked itself by the time I arrived at the lift entrance. I walked back to the reception, explained what had happened, the receptionist patiently released the lift again. I walked a little quicker, jumped in the lift and out of the corner of my eye I could see someone running towards the lift. I scanned the lift buttons to find the Open Doors button, identified the tiny arrows pointing outwards (dear Lift Manufacturers, could you not just paint them GREEN and RED, thanks), hit the button and held the door open for the guy behind me. Turns out he was the examiner, which I didn't find out until a few minutes later.

After the exam I felt a need to have a little stroll, burn off some physical energy, a local market had some pretty dresses, quite unusual. I turned one round that was hanging on a windy market stall only to find the dress had a feather necklace built into the design of the dress through some metal holes in the neck. Another unexpected feather. I thanked the Universe and continued walking through the market where there was another cat sitting in the centre of the market, in East London, clearly waiting to be adored and pandered to.

As I stood and watched the cat, in awe really, at seeing one of my favourite symbols on my Special Day, the second one of the day, a guy walked up to the cat and stroked it, a big cuddle. As if this is something he did every day. The cat didn't scratch him or play up in any way, it just acquiesced to his administrations.

Admittedly on the way home I jumped on a train which went the longest way ever back to Essex, but on the plus side I had a chance to rest, recharge my batteries and recover from the experience of my Big Day Out.

9th May 2017: Sitting down to write some of this book, I had a slurp of tea, a deep breath and hic-cups. I was in a rush to begin, I wasn't being present and I was rewarded with hiccups. I turned on a Youtube video just as Alan Watts was talking about hic-cups or hiccoughs, whichever you prefer, while I was hiccupping.. (Alan Watts Wisdom Channel on Youtube 'By Letting it go, you get the control').

10th May 2017: The day of the full moon. This was an anti-synchronicity day for me. Issues with phone providers for myself and my son, mis-communication between myself and a prospective new employer. There seemed to be more anti-synchronicities than synchronicities. I was not really expecting anything major in my world. A few days earlier I had arranged for a change in mobile phone provider. A change of sim card, a different number. Only temporarily, I had been assured by their website. It was easy. They said. To change a number. I may be without service for a short time. An unquantified, short time. Which turned out to be pretty much most of the day and evening of the full moon.

I put it down to anti-synchronicity in action. I checked if I was feeling out of sorts, what was I doing to make that happen? I spotted the fear and worry in mind, quiet and not at the front of my mind, just in the background, subconsciously, quietly working away about the difficulties that were bound to ensue with the change of a mobile phone provider!

Sure enough, the time it took was much longer than I expected, but nothing life-changing. Having the internet these days is pretty much like having a mobile phone, right? That is right, except my internet provider, an entirely different company, chose today, the day of my mobile phone service vanishing into the ether of website promises, to make improvements to their own service by digging up cables in my street, leading to loss of internet, pretty much all day! I laugh at anti-synchronicities and stick to the 'every cloud has a silver lining' mantra.

11th May 2017: Diana and the butterflies. I have a friend who is a fellow counsellor, a fellow believer in life after death, mediums, psychics, after-death communication in dreams and all sorts of open-minded strangeness. I was walking along the seafront with my friend and two butterflies flew over my head. I exclaimed 'Oh wow, look at the butterflies', despite her beliefs my friend's response 'It's summer, there are butterflies'.

This is how the efforts of the Universe are dismissed, ignored, explained away. For me, the symbolism of the butterfly is one of the most powerful images in the world of personal growth, spiritual development, they are a beautiful reminder of transformation. The grubby caterpillar, slow, furry, beautiful in its own way, struggling, clumsy, effortful and one day the caterpillar emerges, free of the physical bondage it has been encased in and not only is it beautiful to look at, it has wings, freedom of flight, able to fly where it will. What an amazing transformation.

24th May 2017: I had written 24,000 words of this book, I decided to split the document into two separate documents. The synchronicity part of the book and the self-help part. The amount of words in the new document, 11,333, at 12.47. I love the number 11, it reminds me of spiritual awakening, as is triple 3, the number of God and spirit. I also love the randomness of 47 which I have chosen as my special number to pay extra attention to while I am writing this book.

25th May 2017: Taking a little walk for some fresh air along the seafront in Southend. I sat on a bench to take a photo of the high tide and the sun sparkling off the waves only for a little blue butterfly to alight on my handbag. A little visit from one of nature's beauties. Wonderful. I loved it. I thanked the Universe.

25th May 2017: The same little walk, as I was walking uphill, past the Cliffs Pavilion theatre in Southend, a lady was driving her car in a U-turn in a street that had a dead end and there are yellow lines everywhere. She spotted me and wound down her window, I smiled at her, she smiled back. 'Do you know if there is a car park near here?'

I pointed out the giant car park a little further down the hill from where I had just walked. I told her I wished there was a free car park in Southend and we both shared a chuckle as the driver realised there is nowhere to park in Southend, in Summer and definitely not for free. Being Asked for Directions, for me, I am reminded that I am the person who knows the Way.

26th May 2017: Cutting a long story really, really short, I had a series of events drag out over a few weeks, missed meetings because the other person was ill, unnecessary expenses incurred, which I asked to have reimbursed. More delays ensued, a mix up, a promised cheque, then a promise of cash. I was actually paid cash, on the same day I outlaid exactly the same amount of cash on a deposit for room hire for my counselling services, which is a coincidence by itself. The coincidence which felt like it had meaning, the name of the lady who called me to apologise and arrange cash delivery was called Wendy. A coincidental name for me. This list of my own personal coincidences are just to show you, dear reader, how coincidence operates in my little world.

A few days passed, I may have missed writing down the coincidences, it is summer, I saw a few butterflies, a couple of seagulls in unexpected places and a couple of cats. My everyday symbols. How much meaning you give to seeing your symbols is entirely up to you.

For me, because I have been doing this for many years, I acknowledge these symbols and thank the Universe for them, but I no longer write them down. If you are a beginner at understanding the meaning and events around you, write everything down and this is how you will learn which patterns show up for you and when.

30th May 2017: I went along for training for a job involving research. My fellow trainee was called Robert (the name of my brother when he was on the earth plane). Our Trainer told us an interesting story about the founder of the firm I am due to be working for, his name is Bob (the name of my brother now he is in spirit). One of the other trainees joked 'Bob's your Uncle'. I silently thanked spirit for allowing me to be in the position of hearing terms which have meaning for me, at the moment. I am in the middle of writing this book, which I was going to call 'Bob's Your Uncle, Fanny's Your Aunt', but my elderly mother objected and said it is no name for a book.

31st May 2017: Walking home from training with Robert on our second day, a car drove past with the name Rob on the number plate. We both noticed and laughed because earlier in the day we had spoken about the cost of private number plates.

1st June 2017: I am playing the money game with the Universe. Asking the Universe to bring me money, in one form or another, every day. Expected, unexpected, in the form of finding money or having some credit come my way. The Universe is responding, this week, I have had money come to me in the form of cash repayment, literally in the form of actual cash. I had someone call me to see if I would like a free copy of a magazine which would normally cost a fiver, yes please. Today I had an unexpected refund for overpaid postage on a parcel I bought.

2nd June 2017: Coincidental numbers in the amount of money that I spend/receive. I bought some cheese, milk and crisps. Cost: £3.33. It is fun, I enjoy the experience, it is a lovely feeling to be able to notice these synchronicities and know that you are on the right path. Paying attention is the key.

3rd June 2017: I take time out of whatever I am doing, every day, to make sure I have a walk, no matter how little time I can squeeze into my day. So, today the weather was undecided. The sun was out, it wasn't cold, but the clouds were gathering over the estuary and the weather forecasters had threatened torrential rain and risk of flooding.

I headed out, with my son, who was tagging along (he is 24), he is used to me stopping to take photos. My five-minute journey, saw a stopped clock in the park, a giant seagull on our path, an abandoned stripey shirt, and a pair of Hawaiian shorts. We deliberately followed the trail of abandoned clothes and a red admiral butterfly flew across our path. We both enjoyed the moment and managed to be back indoors before the rains came down.

6th June 2017: My first day on my new job, the one I was training for last week. I spent six hours working alongside an amazing 83-year-old, still working and driving. We walked and didn't do much talking, we just got on with the job.

The job involves knocking on doors of the public and asking them for information, to complete an opinion poll. There are many unopened doors or heads which shake, and the feeling of being rejected repeatedly, for me, it is a challenge. I was seeing it as an obstacle to ignore! My supervisor had said to me the day before, let's hope it isn't raining tomorrow. So guess what happened? Yes, it rained, not just a little shower or even a downpour, but a wind-driven downpour with stinging rain and temperatures more suited to Winter than a British Summer.

So, we had been out in the stormy, inhospitable, hostile weather for a good couple of hours when a crow attacked my supervisor. A black crow had been crowing from his tree, his partner was sitting on the gutter of a nearby house. As we walked past, the crow swooped down and body-slammed my supervisor on her cream-coloured woolly bobble hat. I saw it swoop past, she said 'did you see that?' I did see that, my supervisor was a lot shorter than me and the crow smacking full-fat bodyweight onto her head was right in my eyeline.

I was really hoping this event had happened because of her thoughts and it wasn't a sign from my higher self, telling me to let go of this job, right now! It has happened before, it does happen to me, all the things which go wrong. It is almost as if I have jumped onto an anti-synchronicity train to the most wrong job in wrong jobsville and the crow was freaking out about it.

My supervisor began our training telling me this job was hard, really hard, it isn't easy. I got the picture. We set off, expecting it to be difficult. Guess what? It couldn't have been more difficult. We were soaked through, cold, windswept like drowned rats, our clipboards and paper within were all drenched and hardly anyone opened the door.

This combined with a pre-election week, political parties tend to knock on doors, in an attempt to drum up last minute, unexpected support to help swell their ranks. So, we were being mistaken for political campaigners and we were being ignored by a lot of houses.

We headed off to a cafe for a lunch break. My supervisor took off her woolly hat, she had a lump on her head and a bloodstain in her white hair. The crow had drawn blood. I did feel sorry for her, she is such a lovely person and yet here she was, doing her best, thinking the worst and not knowing what she was doing to attract such an event. At 83 I wouldn't expect her to be up to date with the latest thinking about the Law of Attraction or physics or creating your own reality, however, she did say to me, if you think positively about finding someone who will give you a survey, you will find one. I agreed. I felt as though to enter into discussion about the Law of Attraction might be a bit much.

We became more chatty as the day wore on and our pre-set goal of five surveys in one day was in sight, we had achieved three surveys, over half-way, the pressure felt as though it had eased off. As we got to know each other a little more I discovered my supervisor has lived in her house for over sixty years, in an area not really known to me, apart from the fact that my brother lived there when his two little boys were small and I used to visit him (about ten miles away from where I was living).

So, that was the only road I knew in that area. Guess where my supervisor lived? In the exact same road. So, twenty years ago, when I used to visit my brother in his area, I was driving down my supervisor's road. Now it was her turn to drive down my road. I have a feeling that some people's lives are meant to cross. I learnt from my supervisor how to maintain positivity and confidence on a rain drenched doorstep, no matter how cold or dreadfully fed up you want to feel, you force yourself to empty your mind and focus on the matter in hand, the goal, the opening of other people's doors.

The sun came out, the wind died down and a little car with a private number plate caught both of our attention. 'Bob'. I silently thanked Spirit and my Supervisor confided that she enjoyed noticing meaningful number plates.

7th June 2017: I went out working on my own for the first time, knocking on doors and finding people who will answer an opinion poll. I wasn't looking for coincidences, not really. The first person who opened their home to me had two giant black poodles.

I thought back to yesterday, one house had a black poodle called the same name as a little girl I know.. I remembered Spirit and thanked the Universe for helping me find the right door.

I still wasn't completely convinced that I am able to get people to let me into their homes, so I wasn't feeling overly confident, maybe that is why people decided to trust me and to let me in. I let them decide if they want me in their home or not, without doing any sales spiel. I discovered by not having any preconceived idea when I knock on the door, leads to people who are non-judgmental and happy to help, opening the door.

8th June 2017: The day of the General Election, I met a guy whose surname is Luck, lucky by name, lucky by nature. Having a black cat tattoo on my wrist does usually lead to a conversation about Luck, but this is the first time I have met a person actually named Luck.

9th June 2017: I have friends who indulge my belief in Spirit and generally are happy to be dragged along to whatever latest expression of self I have become involved in, whether it is drumming meditation or healing or in this case, being guinea pigs for trainee mediums.

One of my contacts at the church asked if I would like to go along for a free reading, to help the mediums who are learning to give readings and I was welcome to bring a friend. I asked a couple of friends, thinking they probably wouldn't both be free, and yet they were, both free, both able and both willing to join me at the church for an evening of readings. All three of us piled into June's husband's car, it was his birthday! He didn't seem to mind, it was only a short journey to have to contend with three chatting excited women.

The Trainee readers were really interesting. My reader gave me the name Anne and a lovely reading, my son's nan is called Anne, but she was still living and breathing at the time of the reading. My friend June had a reading where she was given a message about cleaning an oven, which she has been given before in a reading. My other friend was asked if the name Sue meant anything to her? My friend said 'Yes, that is my name, and was my mum's name and her mum's name'. We all enjoyed the readings, and the expression of information, wherever it came from.

10th June 2017: I was asked for directions to the church I went to last night. Strolling along in Southend, mid-day, armed with my Survey Clipboard, I was en route to my afternoon shift and a lady walked towards me, smiling, I removed my earphones and smiled at her. If only she knew the significance I place on 'Being Asked For Directions'.

The lady had a northern accent and was clearly from out of the area, she said 'Is there a church near here called St Matthews?' yes, indeed, there is. I gave her directions and took a minute to explain that I had been there last night for readings. The lady explained she wasn't there to go to church, she was there to see a performance by her son, who was studying at the local acting school. I am reminded that I am the person who knows the way.

11th June 2017: My son saw a butterfly being eaten by a blackbird. This cannot be good! For me, this is a friend, represented by the blackbird, doing something to upset him or worse, destroy his current dreams.

11th June 2017: I am paying extra attention to the word's which people use as I meet them on my daily travels. I met a glass re-surfacer. He said 'Prepare to be bored'. With my heightened awareness of the words people are using to me, I replied 'It isn't boring for me'. He said he is a glass re-surfacer. It is only boring for him. He also said 'It's a hard life'. Not in relation to his work, but just generally. I just paid attention.

Once you are aware of the power of words and the effect it has on the person saying them, it is difficult to hear anyone making statements which don't serve them, without feeling as though you are witnessing a human on auto-pilot. Saying words unthinkingly, without being aware of what it means to them and where they are going. It isn't a hard life for everyone, certainly not all the time in all places and even a hard life can be made easier by paying attention to what is working rather than talking about what isn't working.

12th June 2017: Two white cats in separate streets, three feathers, bumped into someone I know (in a town of 250,000 people) and I was asked for directions, to an orthodontist which I had used for my own son ten years ago.

As an interviewer in people's houses, I do meet new people every week, which does put me in a unique position to have new material from people I know nothing about.

14th June 2017: Writing this book, the act of writing about coincidences whilst I am writing this book, is creating coincidences around the writing. When I started writing, I set myself a goal of 1000 words a day and I promised to sit for at least an hour, typing. This first hour often led to 3 or 4 hours of working and the words did appear. As part of my first-class skills in procrastination, I created a spreadsheet setting out the sections of the book and the word count for each section as I went along.

By today I had six sections, with section 4 having 8035 words. I did a little typing on this journal for the coincidences yesterday, and then wrote the wordcount on my spreadsheet for section 4. At first glance I thought I must have the section wrong because I know I have just written some words and yet section 4 already said 8035 words. A quick double take and I realised it was section 5 which is now on 8035 and section 4 was already on exactly the same 8035. A little nod from the Universal forces at work for me to recognise and appreciate.

14th June 2017: Walking past a junior school in the middle of their boisterous end of year sports day, you know the one, the one where parents file past carrying deckchairs, blankets, packets of grapes, sunhats and water bottles to sit and watch a couple of hundred six-year-olds fry in the sun.

A while ago I had written to my mum and I had mentioned how I had never had a coincidence with her name, her real name, which is Sylvia, she doesn't call herself Sylvia anymore. My mum was fed up with people calling her Sylv so she changed her name to Sybil, of course people then called her Syb, which was worse! So now she calls herself her middle name, Eunice. I was strolling past the Junior School just as the teacher was shouting out the names of the next person to be in a race...'SYLVIA...'. I did enjoy the coincidence.

15th June 2017: I was tired. I had a long week. My mind was taking a rest from noticing the coincidences. I have remembered that another good reason for writing down the coincidence in a diary is to see where the moon phases are during your most eventful synchronicities. Find out which phase the moon was in at the time of your birth (for me, I was born on a full moon) and see if that phase is more eventful and holds more coincidences than the other phases.

16th June 2017: I am so fortunate to have a job which involves knocking on people's doors and asking them if they can complete a market research survey. Today I knocked on a door of a man who said a few days ago he had a conversation with his wife about the Polls and how no-one had ever asked them for their opinion and now, here I was, on the doorstep, asking for their opinion.

20th June 2017: I didn't manage any writing, nothing

seemed to be working for me today. Some expectations I had about a recent job, proved to be wrong. The dead birds were definitely a foreboding of bad news. I had three bits of bad news and despite my own knowledge of the Law of Attraction, I found myself feeling lower than I have done for some time. I went out for a walk, and I was 'rewarded' by the Universe, I saw a golden balloon which was a number two, clearly for a second birthday, but it had deflated enough that somehow it looked like a golden question mark. Which was a perfect mirror for how I was feeling. A bit let down!

All is not lost, I enjoyed seeing two pennies, a black feather, a cluster of white feathers which looked as though a bird hadn't gone down without a fight. At 14.44 I saw a lady walking past with a giant bunch of rainbow-coloured balloons.

21st June 2017: A wrong telephone number rang me, a number I called back and was given the recorded message that the number doesn't exist. The number ended in five 1s.11111. I spent the day reminding myself that all I have to do is stay happy and all around me will start improving!

23rd June 2017: Feeling a bit down in the dumps, another favourite expression, I skipped into my local town centre only to bump into the person I have been writing about above, the lady I know who brought me the coincidence about the name Jackie and she was with her daughter, the one whose house I had unknowingly called at on my first day of training for my market research job.

I felt better for having seen them and had a little chat, I was reminded that I am the person who knows the way. I strolled into my usually overworked and busy hairdresser to find an almost empty salon and my hairdresser available for an impromptu cut. We always have a laugh, we did find something to laugh our heads off over.

23rd June 2017: I am enjoying seeing feathers, black feathers, pink feathers, a rainbow-coloured ball, a lovely feather resting on a table on the inside of the therapy centre where I go to have my counselling supervision (as a qualified counsellor part of the continued personal development is to have monthly sessions of supervision).

26th June 2017: Bumping into people I know is one of my favourite things to do, because I have given that event significant meaning. I set out on a day of Market Research Interviews in an area which I don't know very well, Hockley in Essex. I am given a list of specific addresses to find people who are willing and able to complete surveys and answer questions of lots of general subjects. I was a bit unsure about travelling to Hawkwell in Hockley, it is a bit off the beaten track, I don't know the roads and I don't know anyone who lives there. It is not a place I would say is familiar to me. I jumped off the train and headed towards Main Road, Hockley.

I knocked on two doors, one lady let me in for a survey. Which was so nice of her, I am always stunned at people's generosity. The way the computer asks the questions, I do not have to ask for the interviewees name until the end of the survey. So it wasn't until the end of the survey that I discovered this lady is the wife of a Solicitor I used to work for thirty years ago when he had a practice in Leigh on Sea. I enjoyed the coincidence and when the computer asked me the question 'Do you have permission from your supervisor to work outside of your postcode area?' I ticked 'yes', thinking the tablet must be up the swanny.

This was Main Road and I was in Hockley. Not being aware there is a Main Road Hockley and a Main Road, Hawkwell, also in Hockley, I carried on regardless. The next person to invite me in to take a survey turned out to be one of my son's teachers when he was in senior school. Again, I didn't put two and two together until the end of the survey and I asked her name. There was also a lovely coincidence with her house number, but of course, for confidentiality reasons I am unable to share this with you. This lady had also just returned from holiday in Austria. It was this lovely lady who enlightened me about the fact that I was in Main Road in Hockley and not in Hawkwell. That explains it. So, I was in the wrong road, on the wrong path and yet I met two people who I have been connected with in the past.

As I was looking intently at the google map app on my phone, a car pulled over, beeping and waving. My friend who I trained as a counsellor with! We both laughed at the coincidence of seeing each other on a day when, if I hadn't been working, we would have met up in Southend to have a coffee!

Fortunately, my friend is aware of my love of coincidence and we both enjoyed the significance of bumping into each other in entirely unexpected territory.

I continued on my journey, took myself off the confusing Main Road and another road which found three people who were happy to offer a survey, one lady who had just returned from holiday in Devon (where my Mum was living at the time) and one lady who has just come back from visiting her son.

26th June 2017: My train journey began with a little white feather on the floor at my feet as I chose a carriage to step onto. My train journey ended with a little white feather on the floor at my feet of the carriage I chose to step onto.

3rd July 2017: A lady named Sybil, which is also my mum's name. This lady was in her 70s and had only met two people called Sybil in her life, she used to work at a hotel called Renoffs. Having a chat about coincidences, this lady had the number 17 show up in her life, her son's life, her daughter-in-law's life and the other person called Sybil used to work at Renoffs Hotel. My friend's mum, in spirit, called Jackie, (see the coincidences above) used to work at Renoffs. The next person to give me a survey had a little dog called Jackie. Also bearing in mind that I can knock on thirty doors between being given a survey and let into people's houses.

4th July 2017: An Anti-synchronicity day. Lots of things appeared to go wrong, not just for me, but for other people who I know. One person had a ticket for a music gig in London at short notice because they had been let down by someone who had promised to go. Another person is in need of storage after downsizing. Another person is looking for housing after being made homeless.

These are people I know who are having a tough time. I met someone at a bus stop who told me I was on the wrong bus, so I got off the bus only to discover the next bus was the wrong bus as the bus I was on had been the right bus, which delayed the start of my door-knocking exercise. A day full of anti-synchronicities and people giving me short shrift.

29th July 2017: A few weeks have passed, there has

been decorating and making Youtube videos and worrying about not having enough work and money. All the things which I teach against! But, I am human and I too am on the path of learning. Life is a Game; the Game of Life is easier to play if you are the person making the rules.

Also, dear reader, now is a good time to recommend the book 'Game of Life and How to Play It' by Florence Scovel Shinn.

If you are at the mercy of other people and their power games, life does become more of a struggle. I have been continuing to practice the Law of Attraction and to enjoy the appearance of feathers, unexpected and in unusual places, but I consciously decided to change what I am manifesting, and I am going to attract literal cash.

This seems like an impossible task to me. But why should it? Why should money showing up on my path be any less possible than feathers showing up at my feet? I guess the logical side of my mind says, 'Birds don't fly around dropping ten pound notes out of the sky'.

But I decided the theory is stronger than my disbelief. I consciously had a little dig around in my own beliefs about money and what is naturally holding me back. My sense of disbelief, and the gnawing thought that this is never going to happen, don't be stupid, you have now reached a new level of gullibility, the Law of Attraction isn't real, you are never going to have money dropped in your lap, no-one knocks on your door and hands you money. All those sort of thoughts, the sane, rational thinking of the majority of people. The people I know anyway.

Day one of my little experiment and I found a 10p. A little ten pence piece. Wow. I have found many pennies over the years, which I didn't really associate with cash money, I just saw them as a little nod from spirit, you know, a little 'You are in the right place at the right time' type of sign. I cannot remember being given or finding silver coins. I enjoyed the coin, I took a photo, posted it on YouTube, gave thanks to the Universe and put it in my little pot, a miniature treasure chest, the type Pirates used to use. Or maybe they still do!

It wasn't about the value of the ten pence, it was the act of asking for real money and then a real coin showing up. Great. The next day I saw a 20p in the road. I reached down to my feet and picked it up. Lovely. I thanked Spirit. I took a photo, posted it to Facebook, I really should use Instagram but I can't be bothered. Maybe I will begin that path. Skip forward to 2023 and I can be found on Instagram at @taztasticsilver

There I was, strolling along the road in Southend on Sea, in Essex, near a road where I live. This isn't an area where people are likely to be careless with money. There are a lot of impoverished people in this area, as well as having some of the richest people in the country, we also have some of the poorest people in the country. The chances of me finding actual cash on these streets is actually quite low, I would have thought.

Most people who walk the streets are penny conscious and keeping their cash safe. People with money tend to drive safely in their cars. So, there I was, strolling along, as a guy on a bicycle was riding on the road towards me, his jacket flapping in the wind.

As he passed by, I noticed something come into realisation out of the corner of my eye. As I focused on the rectangle of paper which floated down onto the grey tarmac near my feet, but in the road, I made out the unmistakable colours of a ten-pound note. I shouted out to the cyclist, as I stepped into the road to pick it up.

A policewoman, who just happened to be parked on the same street, shouted out to me, to stop me from being run over by a recycling van which was driving towards me. It was at least twenty feet away and I knew he wasn't going to be running me over. He is a recycling van; he is used to crawling along the roads collecting the rubbish.

I re-united the cyclist with his floating tenner, and I stepped back onto the pavement. The recycling van pulled up alongside me and wound his window down. I thought he was going to be telling me off, but no, he shouted at the bloke on the bike:

'That's a really nice thing to do that is, that's rare'.

I shuffled off, torn between embarrassed, shy and agreeing, that yes, he is right. I did a good deed to feel generous and give the tenner back to its rightful owner! At one stage in my life I would have happily picked the money up and strolled off to buy some kettle chips and chocolate éclair cakes and things which I couldn't usually afford to buy.

I shared my story on YouTube and with one of my friends. I love this idea that I was in the right place at the right time to have seen the money manifest on my path and that I was able to notice the money and I was able to call the guy back. There are so many little things to be grateful for in this scenario. Fabulous. I am the person who is in the right place to reunite lost items, lost cash and also to be able to share the story.

A couple of days later, I was sat with one of my friends, making a YouTube video about communicating with spirit and I linked with spirit to bring her images which came to my mind: A cake on a plastic tablecloth, some random images, the things we chatted about, golden balloons, blue balloons, a goat, various symbols and images which we spoke about to remind my friend of a person in Spirit known to her as Pops. I said, how would we see the name Pops? What pops? Obviously balloons pop. So I said we should pay attention to a popping sound and to acknowledge that is a sign from the woman in Spirit called Pops. We both agreed we would try this. We put the television on, having given up trying to link with Spirit directly, nothing happened. There were a set of adverts on, on a pre-recorded programme, we were watching on catch up. The first advert had a cake on a plastic tablecloth. The next advert had some golden balloons, and another advert had a little goat. We laughed at the 'coincidences' and we both enjoyed them. We watched the rest of the adverts intently, looking out for the 'pop', both convinced that we were about to witness some wonderful coincidence. But no, it didn't happen.

The next day, I was out and about, in a card shop with another friend, buying a birthday card. When I took the card out of the bag the shop assistant had put it in I noticed there was a leaflet in the bag. It was an advert for balloons and the word 'pop' was printed on the front! I took a photo and sent it to my friend, who enjoyed the coincidence.

The same friend knocked on my door later that day, holding a folded ten pound note. She handed it to me, I said 'What's this?'. She only found a tenner lying on the floor of the supermarket where she was shopping. She bought it round to me and insisted I take it. She felt that because I was trying to manifest actual cash, this one was definitely meant for me! I tried to insist that she should keep it, but she was having none of it.

One week, two dropped tenners came into my little world. What are the chances?

May 2023: As I edit this book I have notification from a charity that I have won a tenner on their lottery this week. I also gave a tenner to a homeless guy in Southend. I felt as thought I had been paid back by the Universe.

I met someone on my Survey travels who had a sister called Sylvia. My mum was called Sylvia before she changed her name. Someone else on my Survey travels had given up smoking seventeen years ago on August Bank Holiday weekend. My birthday is on August Bank Holiday weekend.

These little coincidences are what we have in common. They may seem inconsequential to anyone reading, as if we all have connections and if you dig far enough you will find something in common with everyone we meet. This could be true, but for me, the information is on the surface, it is one of the first things people say to me, I speak, they speak and five minutes later a coincidental piece of information has emerged.

Another day, my apologies I have no idea what day it was because I dropped my journal off my daily routine. I was out taking market research surveys, armed with my tablet in my backpack and my official-looking clipboard. It was the end of a long day and I needed to find one more Survey (the company ask for four a day, which takes about six hours, to find and complete, and you are only allowed to work for six hours), so I was twenty minutes away from my going home time and I had one more Survey to find.

I carried on knocking on closed doors and I decided on one final door. Each Survey takes about 30-40 minutes, so finding a Survey with only twenty minutes to go, means working for free, which has never appealed to me, so if I didn't get one in this last house, I was going home.

The door opened just as I reached the knocker, a lady was leaving her friend's house. The lady of the house didn't want to do a Survey, but her friend talked her into it. I think her friend was enjoying her company and they sounded like they had been having a laugh working together all day. They had been working together clearing out cupboards full of glassware and crockery, plates, knives and forks and they had lined it all up on a table, where they sat me, with my tablet, having a laugh as we did it.

I started my Survey, and the lady of the house answered my questions, questions about drinking and smoking, and roll ups and where she purchased her tobacco, just as I was typing in the answers, there was a knock at the door and the lady had some tobacco delivered. By hand. From an unknown source. It was literally the question I was asking her at that moment in time, 'Where do you buy your tobacco from?', naturally, she declined to answer the source of the mysterious tobacco deliverer.

We all laughed, and I did the Survey as quickly as possible and left the house. Grateful that her friend had talked her into letting me in and happy to have completed my targets which had been set for me. What are the chances?

A couple of days later I returned to the same street, having another six-hour shift and a further four Surveys to find, only to bump into the lady's friend again, this time she was parked in the street in her Camper Van. She said she could give me a Survey, I could jump in her mobile home, which was parked outside her house. Her house had been flooded and needed work done on it but the insurance didn't want to pay out and so she was having to stay with her neighbour/friend and didn't actually have a home of her own to live in at the moment.

She also told me of how her husband had died after a brain tumour had been wrongly diagnosed as Alzheimer's and it was shortly after her husband died that her home had been flooded. As we sat in her Camper Van, (I use capital letters because I love Camper Vans and my ideal lifestyle involves a Camper Van and a cat), a boy racer flew past, revving his engine in an obnoxious, unpleasant for a Sunday way, far too fast for a residential street like we were on. I said 'That is so irresponsible, if a child ran out, they could be killed with him going so fast'.

She said 'That is what happened to my son, he was five when he ran out and he was knocked down and killed in this road'. We sat quietly for a number of seconds as I digested this information and she was reminded of her lost son. It was a poignant moment for both of us. Her hands flew up to her face, covering her mouth, almost as if she hadn't meant to say that and she didn't know why she had said it. I sat quietly next to her and listened to the story of what happened to the guy who killed her son and how he hadn't been sent to prison for a really long time and how there is still no policing or extreme restrictions of speed on the same street.

I was amazed that she could still be living in the same street, with the same view, every day. She said her Camper Van manages to obscure the view of the street, mainly, so she doesn't have to see what is going on out there.

August 2017: I can only apologise for not keeping a strict journal surrounding the coincidences and weird things that happened to me this month. I sort of fell down the rabbit hole of the Mandela Effect and YouTube videos on the subject, as well as being busy keeping my boss happy and delivering information!

Despite the idea that I know how not to complain, I seem intent on explaining my lack of discipline, and of course, this naturally comes across as complaint. I have also been making YouTube videos about my coincidences that I have been enjoying this year.

As I type this there is a you tube video playing in the background '10 Strange True Glitch in the Matrix Stories' by youtuber Kinspook where he is telling a story about finding a card addressed

'To Tami, all my love Auntie' my name is Tamie, short for Tamasin and I have today written a letter to my aunty Chris. I have to rewind the you tube video to check the story!

The story on YouTube is about a little book of sayings and affirmations, just as I am researching some sayings and affirmations for this book. It does leave chills. When synchronicity happens to you and you find yourself in the centre of a jigsaw puzzle, it can feel weird, but also fabulous!

Two days of walking up and down a street led to the final knock of a door, I really had given up and the lady let me in to do a survey. I do have a black cat tattoo and it is the 13th August, it leads to a conversation about whether a black cat is lucky or unlucky and the number 13. My favourite story is to tell the one about my Dad being born on 13th July, the 13th and final child. The lady tells me her sister was born on 13th October and had two children, 13 years apart, both born on Friday 13th. Okay then. I have a distinct feeling that you are just meant to meet some people.

After discovering that you can search for library books via your home computer, I knocked myself out and ordered all of the Convoluted Universe series. I borrowed four giant books from the library by Dolores Cannon and promised myself I would have them read and done and dusted within a few weeks.

However, a few days passed, one of the books was picked up, put down, opened, closed, time came and went and before I knew it, three weeks had elapsed, I don't know where the time went, but I needed to renew the Dolores Cannon books. I logged on to the local library system, how fantastic is that? Only to find that I could not renew my book because someone else wanted to read them and they had reserved the book.

I trotted to the library to return the book, because

returning a book to the library past the due date is a crime punishable by a fine. Monetary loss no less. Since I had no intention of parting with cash unnecessarily, I was keen to take the book back.

While I was in the library I had a browse of their merchandise section, they often sell little knick knacks, collectibles if you will, and you just never know when you will need some birthday gift wrapping paper covered in cats reading books. Or world maps. You get the picture.

The local library is eclectic in its appreciation of selling toot. The levels of toot cover all bases and I am pretty sure there is something for every one of their readers based on their reading preferences. Google must go wild on the analytics of library users. So I browsed.

My mum has a birthday in August, but she is very difficult to buy for. If I get it wrong, I get it in the neck. My mum will literally complain about birthday cards I have sent to her, if she doesn't find it funny or it is not to her liking. I have to play it safe. I want to play it safe. I don't want to upset her.

I find a little brooch in the 'Remember The Tudors' section which is symbolic of the Tudors, a silver feather. Plus, my mum has recently told me that gold looks cheap, and as a Virgo, I shouldn't wear gold, she prefers silver. Clearly the symbolism of the feather has deeply spiritual connotations, angels, guardian angels, spirit guides, I will send her a silver feather brooch.

I am learning how it feels to have 'help' from spirit. It is like operating on automatic pilot. Acting and going with the flow which feels like a breath from behind, not windy, not a draught, but far gentler than that, not even as heavy as breath, lighter than a feather, you just find yourself doing things without even needing to give it a second thought. That is the only way I can explain it. You don't need to run it through your logic filter, your 'Is it for the best' filter, or 'What will the possible consequences of my actions be' filter. There is no need for a filter, it looks right, it feels right, it is right. I posted my mum a non-funny, nothing to be offended by birthday card and the silver feather brooch.

Much to my delight my mum wrote to say she had heard from her sister, my aunty Chris, who had reminded her of a silver feather brooch my mum had given to her when they were younger and how my aunty Chris still had the brooch!

Then my mum received my brooch through the post. So, I was buying the brooch as my aunty Chris was writing to my mum. My mum phoned me to check when I posted the silver brooch to her! She could hardly believe that this little string of coincidences had happened. It was not really a surprise to me, but I was thrilled that both my mum and my aunty Chris had also been touched by spirit. What prompted my aunty Chris to write about the silver feather brooch? What prompted my mum to write to me about it?

My mum sent me a business card that she had picked up from a medium in Devon. My mum sent it to me to show me an example of what I could do on a business card. I sent it back to her, attaching my own business card I had printed for my Counselling practice. The design of my card? You guessed it, a butterfly design, via Vistaprint, identical to the one my mum had picked up.

I started going to church regularly this summer, mainly to drag one of my friends along who has never been to spiritualist church before, and it is always fun to introduce someone else to new experiences. We went along, my friend was given a message, she was given the name Poplar, I thought it was because the woman she had in spirit was called Pops, but when she got home she checked with her brother if there was a link to Poplar in London, only to discover their childhood home had been called Poplar.

Also, the blue balloons keep showing up on my path. Three in one day last week. A partly inflated blue balloon that was floating on my path, it hadn't been knotted up. A partly deflated blue leather football, which, to all intents and purposes looked like a blue balloon, followed by a woman leaving the local Wok &

Go who were giving away blue balloons for free, armed with no less than five blue balloons balanced all around her child's buggy.

I was also handed a balloon by a small child, who thought I had dropped it. Which was sweet of him, and I should have taken it from him to make him feel he had given it to the right person, but I had actually seen who had dropped it, a small boy whose mum did not have time to chase a balloon he had dropped. I pointed out the correct owner and the little boy went running off in the right direction to find the rightful owner of the balloon.

The Rose. The Reading at Church Story

I had offered to do a reading at my local spiritualist church. At the end of the last service, the lady who runs the church asked if anyone wanted to do a reading of any description. This is usually reading some form of spiritual story, or something from the Bible. I offered and set about thinking about what I should read. I settled on the lyrics to the song 'the Rose'. I was going to stand up on the podium and read these words:

Some say love, it is a river
That drowns the tender reed
Some say love, it is a razor
That leaves your soul to bleed
Some say love, it is a hunger
An endless aching need

I say love, it is a flower
And you, its only seed

It's the heart, afraid of breaking
That never learns to dance
It's the dream, afraid of waking
That never takes the chance
It's the one who won't be taken
Who cannot seem to give
And the soul, afraid of dying
That never learns to live

When the night has been too lonely
And the road has been too long
And you that love is only
For the lucky and the strong
Just remember in the winter
Far beneath the bitter snows
Lies the seed that with the sun's love
In the Spring becomes the Rose.
(Source: Musixmatch)

They seemed like the perfect words to offer as my first 'reading' in front of a congregation. I changed my mind at the last minute and decided to tell one of my favourite jokes instead. Just as well I did change my mind, because when I got to church, the song that the congregation were being asked to murder that week was 'The Rose'.

To me, that is the Universe having a laugh. Can you imagine if I had rocked up and opened my little bit of paper and read out the words to the song everyone had just sung! Maybe that would have been funnier than the joke I told instead.

Later that week, on my actual birthday, as I was walking to a counselling session I saw a rose on my path. A lovely pink rose. I thanked Spirit and recognised how fortunate I am to have this experience.

A pink balloon with the words 'big birthday' written on in large letters, blew across my path during my birthday weekend. Birthdays do seem to attract more coincidental offerings from the Universe. I saw two beautiful white feathers, one on my path and one inside the doorway of the library.

As I made a YouTube video re-telling the story of the Police cars which appeared and disappeared as if on cue. My mum wrote to me reminding me of the time I saw Police cars from Spirit. I have no idea what caused her to write to me about that incident. We do not speak on the phone regularly, or use text messaging, my Mum does not use computers or even email. So, for her to write to me about the story I had just published a YouTube video about, was indeed quite out of the blue coincidence.

Joke for Church

What's that, dear reader? You want to hear the joke I stood up and told at Church? Okay then. Are you sitting comfortably?

One day there was a huge flood and a guy, let's call him Matt, had to climb on his roof to escape the water.

He prayed to God:

'Save me God, I have faith that you will save me'

A fire engine came driving through the rapidly rising waters and the fire brigade shouted at Matt to let them save him.

'No thanks' Matt waved them away, 'God will save me, I have faith'. The fire engine drove away.

A neighbour came past in his rowing boat and offered Matt a space in his boat. 'Jump in' he offered.

'No thanks' Matt refused, explaining 'God will save me, I have faith'.

Matt's neighbour rowed away.

A helicopter circled around Matt's roof, waving and offering Matt help.

'No thanks' Matt refused, 'God will save me'.

The waters continued to rise, Matt drowned and went to heaven. As he was shaking the water off, he asked God accusingly 'I had faith that you would save me, where were you?'

God said: 'I sent a fire engine, a rowing boat and a helicopter, what more did you want?'

It went down well and the whole church laughed, but I haven't been asked to do a reading since.

Finding Coins Story

August also brought many coins on my path. 40p on a day when I really needed a drink and I thought I had put a few pound coins into my backpack, turns out, I forgot to empty my purse out, from my handbag, into my backpack, one little task I forgot led to thirsty work for me, as I knocked on doors and pounded hot pavements without a drink.

I found 40p by the side of one of those telephone exchanges. I can only imagine the telephone engineer must have bent down to work at one and some coins had fallen out of his pocket, or maybe a teenager had been sitting on the 3ft high, nice and conveniently placed rectangular box, and perhaps the coins had fallen out of their pocket. 40p to me, on that hot, dry, sunny day was exactly the amount of money I need to buy a can of cream soda on the way home.

My birthday cards arrived, three in the post on the same day, all with butterfly pictures on the front.

Being asked for directions – a man wanted to know where Clifftown Parade was. Bumping into people, met some people I hadn't seen for over a year, a lady from church who doesn't live in this part of town and then a lady from the volunteer centre.

I had a job interview with a guy in Romford, when I came home I put the telly on and a Youtube video popped up with the exact same name as the guy I had just interviewed with.

October 2017: Many days and weeks have passed, I am thinking that you have read enough of my personal coincidence journal, so I haven't shared every coincidence that showed up. However, I think this particular coincidence is worthy of a mention. One of my son's female friends turned up unexpectedly. I was chatting with her about my book, Born Under Lucky Stars, published in October 2017 and how I am writing my next book about coincidence. As we were talking her phone rang, she let it ring and she listened back to the voicemail.

It was from her aunty:

'Your dream came true, you were right, I am ten weeks pregnant'.

Clare had dreamed that her aunt was pregnant, she had messaged her to tell her about her dream, and as we were talking about coincidence, her aunt chose that exact moment to confirm her dream.

I would call that an example of synchronicity.

November 2017: I am still taking photos of objects which show up on my path, expected or unexpected. I do enjoy keeping the record, sharing to Facebook with a little text to remind me what the coincidence was and what it all meant to me at the time.

As you become more adept at learning to communicate with the Universe, you will learn to a) really pay attention to words people say to you and events which happen around you and b) act, depending on your own interpretation of those things.

I often notice messages from Spirit during times of stress, possibly because I am feeling a greater 'need' during those times. A few days after being offered a new job, I was walking on my regular shopping trip, a couple of miles up the road to visit a cheap store where everything is at least 10p cheaper than anywhere else and I saw an abandoned 'L' plate on a wall of a house. I took a photo, for my 'Unexpected sights' album on Facebook.

A couple of days later, in preparation for a week at work, I took the walk to the shop again, this time for sustenance during my working week, bottled water, biscuits, generally stuff to keep me going. I noticed the 'L' learner plate was still there, only this time it had been joined by an abandoned hat! The hat, for me, symbolizes a hats off from the Universe. You know the saying 'Hats off to you' in olden times when people were used to wearing hats, they would tip their hat in your direction by way of saying 'hello'. It is also a way of acknowledging an achievement, a qualification, another level of success. Hats off from the Universe is a little pat on the back, confirmation that you are heading in the right direction. Well done, keep going.

I started my new job, surrounded by data, in a retail store with all manner of text on goods, labels, posters, notices, product packaging, Christmas stock, cards, banners, the list is never ending and changes on a weekly basis. The first week, the store has a stand dedicated to little Christmas badges with people's names on them, so Santa can identify who the people are, a little red Christmas wreath with a name written on it.

Festive, fun, cheap as chips. I spent a few hours every day looking at that stand, sorting the names and putting them back in the place they belong. The stand next to it had more names on it, just like car number plates, but for door labels or to simply stick on a wall of a bedroom. The name 'ALFIE' had fallen and was hanging in the wrong slot, I made a big deal of putting the right name where it was meant to be, my new work colleague, who had started on the same day as me, said 'That's my nephew's name!' I told her I love coincidences like that. I am reminded of being surrounded by Spirit and as I am working and learning a new till, a new routine, new procedures, I 'call on' spirit to bring me strength, peace, calm and tranquility to help me in my new role.

Walking to work the next day, a car number plate with three sixes on, the number I associate with harmony and abundance. Let the Good Times Roll.

At work: being asked the time by a customer. The time, 3.21. I do love to be reminded of the time and being asked for the time. It acts as a reminder to me to live in the now. Right here, right now, is the only time we ever have.

25th November 2017: One month until Christmas Day, it is a beautiful sunny, crisp, cold, Autumn on the cusp of winter day. Although I have a cold which I have picked up from my retail co-workers, who in turn are blaming the sneezing customers.

I feel the best way to stay well, is to take my cold outside and enjoy as much of the day as I can. I walk, briskly, smiling at the sun and enjoying the day. This does generally bring about smiles from other people, smiling is much like yawning, anyone who crosses your path cannot help but smile, even if it is to themselves. Up ahead of me on my path, I can see a beautiful golden, brown furred Alsatian, sitting patiently on the cold grey pavement, while her elderly woman has a rummage in her handbag.

'What a beautiful dog you have' I say as I walk past, taking one earphone out of my ear, in case she does respond by speaking.

'It's her birthday today'. I have to go back to check I have heard correctly; I haven't slowed down my pace so I have walked past two or three paces before the old lady replied.

I stroll back, smiling, stroking her dog and repeating 'Her birthday!' 'Yes, she is 12 today'. I delight in this coincidence. It really pleases me to be able to share the news with this woman about her baby, and the idea that dogs have birthdays is just fantastic, to meet a dog, on its birthday is also added joy.

Returning from my walk I pass a door which has a new number painted on, in giant numbers. Number 147. This is the number at the end of my mobile phone number and one of the first numbers I started paying attention to for this book.

I cannot stress the effectiveness of keeping a written record of the coincidences. The reasons I say this are twofold, firstly in order not to forget the coincidence, they can be so fleeting, like a dream, they can be easy to forget, secondly, the act of writing the coincidences down does solidify your commitment to receiving messages from the Universe.

The happier you are and the more grateful you are to receive personal info direct to your little world, the more the Universe will communicate with you.

Coincidental numbers continue: Watching 'Man Down' on television, a sitcom with Greg Davies, one of my favourite actors, he does make me laugh. I haven't had a tv licence for months, but leading up to Christmas, there were a lot of tv programmes that I liked the look of. What with the cold weather and a love of using television to spot coincidences, a wealth of information flooding into our homes on a daily basis, I relented, and bought a tv licence.

You know that feeling when you haven't had something for a while, like, say, chocolate, or coffee, something you really love, and then you are given full access to as much of it as you want? Well, that is what put me in front of 'Man Down' on television. I switched the programme on randomly in the middle of a show only for Greg Davies to be explaining to have been kidnapped and padlocked. His captor was giving him the number to his padlock, for him to free himself. The number? 1805. Greg's birthday, 18th May.

The coincidence here, for me, is that in this book I

have a whole story about the bloke who shows up from the ONS to do a survey, his birthday was also on 18th May. But, the coincidence, in this instance, just served as another prompt for me to hurry up and finish my book.

30th November 2017: I was tweeting about Oscar Wilde and how he looks like Jonathan Ross. I don't know why I felt I had to follow that up and have a little google, but I did, only to discover that I was looking Oscar Wilde up on the anniversary of his death in 1900. **Beginning of December 2017**: A race towards Christmas, which has been in the shops since the day after Halloween. I do have a foster cat I look after, a grey Persian, called Pumba. He is a beautiful cat, you couldn't wish for a nicer natured pet, and I love to look after him for his owner, who is a friend of mine, who rescued him from homelessness after I posted his picture on Facebook!

So, I feel like a surrogate owner to Pumba and he holds a special place in my heart. I haven't looked after him for a couple of months and I miss him. I was walking along the street, and I noticed a ginger cat, a giant, fluffy, Persian-like ginger cat who was walking towards me. I whipped out my phone and took his photo, because this is also one of my hobbies, as a serious collector of coincidences and a lover of symbolism, I do like to share the symbols which show up for me, and for me, a ginger cat is one of them.

I have assigned the ginger cat, specifically, to act as a

reminder of Spirit in our daily lives, whenever I see a ginger cat, I send a thought to my spirit guide, and I pay attention to whatever I have to feel really grateful for. By coincidence, my postwoman walked towards me, at exactly the moment I was taking a photo, explaining about the ginger cat. His owner has left the country and the cat is always outside in the cold because the lodger is out at work all day.

We commiserated and the postwoman showed me which house the cat is supposed to live in, I told her I would pay them a visit one evening to see if they want to get rid of the cat, in my direction. The postwoman told me the name of the cat. He is called Simba. What are the Chances? Pumba and Simba!

Early December 2017: Battling against lousy weather, I was walking through Southend Town Centre, fighting with my umbrella which was determined to go along with the wind. A lady approached me, with no umbrella and cold water splattering on her face. I held my brolly over both of us as she said 'Southend Train Station?' I pointed her back down the High Street, the Central Train Station which heads into Fenchurch Street. 'No' she corrected me 'I am going to Rayleigh'.

Oh, the train line which heads into Liverpool Street Station, okay then, back the way I had come, and across a set of traffic lights. She must have had a rough idea of where she was going, and needed a little reassurance that she was in fact heading the right way. I don't blame her, who wants to waste their time walking the wrong way in icy rain? But for me, the lover of Life Events, such as Being Asked for Directions. I am reminded that I am writing a book about coincidence and that I really should be getting on with it!

The weather has taken a turn for the worse. Knocking on doors, asking for surveys does feel like a thankless task. Every homeowner is telling me 'No' and I am losing heart. I knock on a door with a beautiful green door and a Christmas wreath of holly, ferns, sprayed with fake white snow. A young man opened the door, full of joy, happiness and energy, he smiled at me and explained kindly that he cannot do a survey because it is his girlfriend's birthday today and they are in the middle of a family gathering.

I didn't feel disappointed, I enjoyed the coincidence, wished his girlfriend a Happy Birthday and bounced off, lifted by the coincidence. The next house I knocked at let me in, gave me a survey, which I think was because I was sharing the happy energy from the previous house!

12th December 2017: Twelfth of the twelfth. What could happen today? Well, my son's nan asked him to help her take some chairs to the local tip. She took so long getting to our house to pick him up that I was ready as well. The timing lined up for me to be able to have a lift into Leigh on Sea, the postcodes I had been assigned for taking Surveys about politics, smoking, drinking and general questions about various other matters. We agreed to meet up at lunchtime for a meal at the local pub, which offered a two for one deal.

I went into a house and took a survey, a beautiful house, with two small children, both of whom have a birthday this week. (I love that coincidence). My phone runs out of battery, so after knocking on a whole street of doors and only finding one survey and being unable to text my son or his nan, I hoofed it round the corner to the local pub and there they were, having a lovely pub lunch, so I joined them.

I tucked in, I enjoyed the lunch. The cost was £7.49 and so the change I was given was £2.51. 251, a number which has shown up a lot for me in the past, by way of a bus number and a house number I lived in. I enjoy the coincidence, I shared it with my companions and thank the Universe for the experience.

Watching an old television programme. I do love the programmes where they go hunting through antiques stores and boot sales, they find a piece of collectible rubbish, barter with the stall holder and then take it to auction to make a few quid. They rarely make a profit, but the whole show is fun to watch. Today's show, the guy found a didgery doo. He bought it and decided he was going to play 'Dancing Queen' on it! I love that coincidence. Just as I am writing and explaining the significance of that song, for me.

Watching a clip of David Jason on a show where he is tracing his roots and uncovering something historical. He shows a list of people, created after the First World

War, an ancient document dated 1919 is on my telly. The date? My birthday. I thank the Universe for the coincidence. I wasn't watching the show, I was channel hopping and that is what showed up on my telly.

13th December 2017: I am doing market research for a living. I find myself knocking on all sorts of doors and meeting all sorts of people. Of course, it is an amazing source of information for me to mine for coincidence. I don't pry, because it isn't part of the job, but often, the coincidence just pops up.

Today's coincidence is that I am interviewing a man in his house, which he built, he had the choice of putting a number on his house, 9,11 or 13. He chose against the number 13 and his house became number 9. It is the 13th today and I have a history with the number 13! He chose against the number 13. I love the idea that he was prompted to share this story with me on the 13th.

14th December 2017: As I am a master procrastinator, combined with being a little lazy, it will come as no surprise to you, dear reader, to hear that whenever I start writing a new book, I use an old template. I 'save as'. Guilty as charged. I am writing a further self-help book, 'Taming Your Negative Dragons'. So I saved as, re-named and actually went as far as to delete all the copied information from my mum's book which I am in the process of editing and proofreading. This is how lazy I am, I deleted all the previous wording, apart from the first line on each page.

It does look a bit weird to start writing on a blank page and to have the first sentence already there, it just sort of helps me to picture the words on the page. My mum's book was sitting on my computer, next to a document waiting for me to type words on. Randomly it was opened at Chapter 10, with just the first sentence still there.

I heard from a friend of mine who had sad news that her brother had been found dead in his flat, he was only around 50, not old enough to die, and yet here was the news of his death. His name was Lawrence. I offered my condolences and eventually, after texting and processing and a few prayers I made it back to the computer. My document was still sitting open. The words read:

'Aged thirty, Lawrence was living with his father.'

I enjoyed the coincidence, I sent a prayer to Lawrence and carried on offering support to his sister. These things happen so often to me now that I am no longer surprised by them, I just accept the coincidence as a little 'hello' from spirit.

15th December 2017: As I am editing a book for my mum, I have the telly on in the background. An actress who has played in the Bill and on Eastenders, is having a go at Celebrity Antiques Road Trip, I look up in time for her to say 'You can call me Rob'. They have a little joke, a pun, a play on words about her robbing him. For me, the name Rob is significant in that this is the name of my brother, now in spirit.

As I am sucked into the programme, which I do love because of the history of the towns they visit. They have a still picture on the screen, it is a photo of an old theatre with a play called 'Tammies Twisters'. My name is Tamie for short, Tamasin for long. I posted a photo of a green balloon to twitter today, 'unexpected twists' was my caption, because the balloon was twisted in knots. I love this sort of coincidence.

Up until this point, I usually have blue balloons show up, so this green balloon, half twisted into some sort of balloon animal was unexpected. As we are heading towards a new moon and we have a couple of days in the dark of the moon, this is a time to expect the unexpected.

Watching another celebrity Antiques Road Trip, the auctioneer was called Lawrence.

18th December 2017: I opened the tarot cards for a friend of mine whose brother Laurence has just died. The reading offered a card with the image of an eagle. Laurence had a stuffed eagle in his home. I did a spirit writing for Laurence's sister, before she came round.

I focus on the person who is in spirit, in a semi-meditative state and write down any words which come to mind. I wrote down PRIME and BLUEBELL, and BLUE, Blue Boy, a name beginning with H, and I saw Laurence in my mind's eye wearing a great sweatshirt and grey tracksuit bottoms.

When my friend came round, she said she was waiting have something delivered from Amazon PRIME, a DVD of Laurence's favourite film which she is going to put in his coffin. The colour Blue is significant for her but it is a little too personal for me to share that information here. The word Bluebell had significance because my friend was going to call her daughter Bluebell and her mum said 'No. Absolutely not'. Her mum is also in spirit, and I felt, together with Laurence. The H name is the name of her son, which I won't share with you here, to protect his anonymity.

My friend also turned up for her reading with a flat tyre. She called out the rescue service who said it was likely to be three hours before anyone could come out. We settled down to read the cards, and after an hour and a half, after the Angel Cards had been read, and the tarot cards and some beautiful cards by Patrick Gamble as a spread to predict 2018, there was a knock on the door, and it was the rescue vehicle. My friend was towed off to have her tyre changed.

A little while later she sent me a message with a photo of Phil Collins on the front of a CD 'Not Gone Yet', which is the phrase we both had in mind thinking about her brother, it is as though he is still around. The coincidence for me is that in the picture, Phil Collins was wearing a grey-coloured hoody.

A couple of days later, my friend was travelling to see

her brother's ex-partner, LOLA. She was driving behind a white Range Rover, the number plate read LOLA and some numbers. What are the Chances? It has to be more than a coincidence.

Leading up to Christmas 2017 was a particularly stressful time for me. A move was in the air, and yet not quite settled, or formalised, with not just a lack of plan as to housing for January 2018, but literally with no idea at all of where I was going to be living in the next few weeks. It was a horrible feeling, being faced with uncertainty on a six-monthly basis. This is what lack of money and focusing on lack brings. So, I have had a test of faith, I carried on.

I kept walking each day, paying attention to the metaphysical objects and items that crossed my path. Pink flowers started showing up. So, the week I heard of Laurence's death, I noticed four pink roses, nearly dead, discarded outside someone's house that I knocked on to ask for a survey. I have never seen four pink roses before, discarded, all lined up like that. Their forlornness, their abandonment in the face of their fading beauty, drew my attention.

This week, I noticed a Christmas wreath on a door, it was adorned with pink roses! Again! How strange. It is a strange choice of colour and flower to put on a Christmas wreath, but there it was. Naturally, as is second nature to me now, I took a photo, and posted it to Facebook to share with everyone else who likes to share my love of coincidence.

Christmas Eve 2017 saw me in the Right Place at the Right Time:

I love talking to people and enjoying all situations, even if it is an apparent problem at the till, or in a queue at a travel centre, or wherever retail occurs, there usually tends to be a clump of humans. Have you noticed that? If someone is querying or making a complaint which involves the person serving to use up more than one person's allotted service time, that is the time when more people will show up who also need serving at that exact moment.

I had a fantastic experience in a Supermarket on Christmas Eve. I decided that I 'needed' some frozen Yorkshire Puddings. The truth of it is, I didn't need Yorkshire Puddings at all. I wasn't having a roast dinner on Christmas Day, but I can always use Yorkshires, probably on Boxing Day, or the day after. I just felt like joining in the last-minute rush of Christmas shopping in the Supermarket. At least, I think it was a mere whim. Of course, it could have been The Universe, since I have offered myself up to be of service to others, it is often when I look back I wonder if I was prompted by an intelligence higher than myself, to take action.

On my way to the local Supermarket on Christmas Eve, I was paying particular attention to events and people around me. I had felt that I was needed somewhere even though I didn't know where exactly, I had put my trainers on, my winter coat, my iPod, grabbed a carrier bag and headed out. I noticed a woman in her sixties reversing to and fro out of a car park space.

As I walked past, I caught her eye and said 'Have you got yourself stuck?' smiling, she looked at me, all flustered and she said 'Yes, yes I think I have'. The lady had a little car, parked in-between two cars on the forecourt of a Christian Bookshop, she had a passenger who just about fit into the little car, with a young teenager also in the back of the car. I asked her if she would like me to guide her out. She asked if I would, I caught a slight Irish accent and walked to the back of the car.

The car had to be reversed between a lamppost and a telephone cable box, whilst missing the two cars parked either side of it. The lady reversed towards me with me telling her when to turn the steering wheel, but she just couldn't seem to understand what she needed to do with the car. I offered to drive it for her. 'Would you?' she said, relieved. Of course. I jumped into the car, tried to the put the car in gear. Nothing. No gears that I could feel. I couldn't even get the car into first gear. I swapped places with the lady, we tried again. It was quite frustrating watching her move the car a few feet and then drive it back to the same place she had been in a moment ago.

She jumped out again, we swapped places again. I

reached for the gear stick, but the passenger's leg was literally leaning on the gear stick. I asked her if she would mind jumping out so I could see out of the window. I managed to move the car forward, but I just could not get the gear stick to shift into reverse.

The lady jumped in for the final time and we tried again, after I had given her precise instruction as to what she needed to do to get her car out. I even stood at the back of her car, with her, for her to get a different perspective on the gap she needed to drive through.

The lady was becoming increasingly flustered, pink in the face and a bit shaky. I kept reassuring her that she could do it, a little bit at a time, she would do it. My positive affirmations seemed to help, and she reversed her car completely out of the space, her passenger climbed back in, we all wished each other Merry Christmas and she drove off. Free from her self-imposed prison of thinking her car was bigger than it was.

I continued my journey, she thanked me profusely and called me an Angel, even though I hadn't been the one to actually drive her car out of the tight spot she had driven it into, she felt as though my presence had been enough to help her do it herself. Sometimes that is all it takes, having someone who is offering to help, even though you don't actually take them up on their offer. Knowing they are there for you if you need them, is enough for you to do it yourself.

Well, whatever or wherever the source of my decision making, I found myself in a Supermarket in front of a giant frozen food section with empty containers. Containers which should have held 50-60 packets of Yorkshire Puddings, was empty. I walked to the customer service counter, at the end of the store, to find a queue, of two. There was a man being served and he was trying to organise a refund on his car parking fee.

The Supermarket charges for parking and if you spend more than a fiver in the store, you can claim the parking back off your shopping at the till. Well, this guy had forgotten to hand over his car parking ticket to the checkout operator and had only remembered after they had passed through the checkout and he didn't want to hold the queue up, so he headed for the customer service counter, while his wife hoofed back to their car with the shopping.

Only problem was, she had taken the receipt for the shopping with her and naturally, the customer service couldn't give him a refund for his parking without the receipt. I had a laugh about it, he had one job and yet he found himself at the counter without the one piece of paper that he needed.

The woman behind me didn't find it funny at all and was clearly upset at having her time wasted. She wasn't quite sure how to respond to my humour. It didn't compute for her in this situation, where clearly, the expected response is anger, frustration and generally offering a vibration of displeasure.

I, however, as a Master (or Mistress) of choice over my own vibrational output, was still thoroughly enjoying the moment. I made it to the till and asked the young lady if there were any frozen Yorkshire Puddings hiding anywhere. She got on the phone and rustled some up. I said I would go off and do some shopping and come back. I went off and minded my own business, mainly, for the remainder of my shopping trip. That is until I had purchased some bits and pieces, whizzed through the self-service checkout, without complaining once, back to the customer service to check on the Yorkshire situation.

I queued again, sort of, a double queue simultaneously appeared, and no-one was really sure which queue was first, until a man pushed his way through the crowd waving a pack of frozen Yorkshires in the air, looking desperately at the customer service assistant, pleading with her to point out which customer wanted them! Me! It was me! I felt like a bridesmaid catching flowers at a wedding. The lightweight Yorkshires came my way. I strolled off towards the lottery counter, relieving the young girl of having to ring up my Yorkshires, I would pay for them elsewhere.

My presence having the effect of splitting up the double queue and causing everyone standing behind me to have to join the other queue. The lottery counter was being served by a guy dressed as the Grinch, which made me laugh, I told him he looked great, which led to him doing a little Jim Carey impression, telling anyone within earshot that he was in fact, fabulous!

The woman in front of me was having a problem with her purchase, she had been 'overcharged', but not really, she had picked up the more expensive item and now wanted a refund. Easy mistake to make. There I was, patiently, waiting behind her. Not angry, not frustrated, just playing my part at being a calm shopper, there to be of service to others.

As I walked home, I was grateful for all the experiences I had in the shop and I was vaguely aware of all the other shoppers who came behind me who had access to their expected frozen Yorkshires, because I had bothered to ask for them to be refilled. There were probably loads of stressed-out Mums, Dads and families, having to shop on Christmas Eve, for a variety of reasons, whose lives were made a little less stressful because of the Yorkshire Puddings.

I wasn't honestly thinking along those lines when I did my good deed for the day, I was literally just thinking that I wanted to buy some Yorkshires. It was almost as though the Universe had propelled me on a mission. I was doing this task for Big Brother. It had to be done. No matter what. I have no idea who was affected by my actions, and maybe I never will know, but what I have learned is not to ignore any prompting. Particularly seemingly random prompting.

25th December 2017 I am sharing one last journal entry with you, dear reader, as a reminder of how The Universe lines us up to be in the Right Place at the Right Time to be of service to others.

Acts of Service. The Universe is going to be delivering ways for me to be of service to others. Because that is what I have been thinking about.

Thinking about the timing of being able to help, how can I be of service to others? There are so many ways. This Christmas Day was a particularly stressful time for me. I am due to be moving, from a rented flat, into…fill in your own conclusion. I guess another rented flat, but as at Christmas Day, there was no new address in sight. There was no room at the Inn. Christmas Day, my 24-year-old son went round to his dads for dinner with his nan and I spent the day in solitary confinement. Which, for me, is quite a pleasure. I love spending time on my own, it leaves me feeling refreshed and ready to face the world again.

Some people are energized by socializing and spending time in busy, noisy environments, personally, I enjoy peace and quiet and spending time in nature. Christmas

Day lunchtime arrived, and I hadn't been out for any fresh air or exercise.

I decided that I would take the over-buttery mince pies, which my son had rejected because they didn't taste quite right, and I don't like mince pies at all, and I would take the uneaten pies and throw them to the seagulls, crows, pigeons, squirrels and probably some rats or whatever other little creatures were to be found in my local park.

I packed the mince pies into a carrier bag. Check list at the door, phone, keys, mince pies. I didn't need my purse or handbag; I was only going to be five minutes. I had also bunged in a half-eaten sausage sandwich into the carrier bag. A cold wind blew in my face and tried to tear the bright orange carrier bag out of my hands.

I reached the park and threw the sausage sandwich near the bin, walking a few steps, I tipped one of the mince pies out of the tin foil case, onto the grass. I checked the sky to see if any birds had noticed that I was there. I put the first tin foil pie holder back into the carrier bag. I took another mince pie, the wind filling my carrier bag as I tossed the pie a few feet away from the first one.

Experience has taught me that if you put all the food in one place, the fat, greedy, strongest birds get all the food. I like to spread it out to give the smaller birds a chance. I put the tin foil case back in the carrier bag, continuing my journey along the concrete pathway.

Seagulls begin to circle overhead; I can feel the cold spray of water from the water fountain in the centre of the park.

Despite the noise of the wind, the noise of the carrier bag blowing and the crows cawing, the call of the seagull is still loud and clear enough to draw the attention of at least a dozen other seagulls. I carried on dropping mince pies onto the grass, until all five were waiting to be eaten. The fifth mince pie was stuck in the foil case, I prised the pastry loose from the foil, shaking the pie onto the ground. A gust of wind blew into my carrier bag, lifting the tin foil cases out of the bag and blowing them all over the ground in front of me.

I rushed around, picking them up from the ground with seagulls circling overhead, cawing, impatient to get to the food, and waiting for me to move out of the way. I retreated to a wooden bench, sitting down to record the birds on my phone. Feeding wild animals is an act of grace, the animals can't thank you or pay you back, and it feels really good to be the provider. So I enjoyed myself.

As I left the park, I walked past a pigeon who had snaffled a whole slice of bread covered in tomato sauce, I paused to watch him/her really enjoy their find. I had popped out on Christmas Day with just my house key, my phone and a carrier bag with food. I didn't need my handbag or my purse, I wasn't expecting to be needing them. Although I did have a packet of tissues in my pocket, this is one of the ways I am able to help other people, by providing the tissue when they are crying! Of course, by having the tissues on me, the argument is, the person who needs the tissue will be brought to me. I am attracting people who need a tissue. I walked back home, still warm from the sense of giving to the birds.

I do love the timing, which of course, for the Universe, is mere child's play, but for me, it is something to be admired and stood in awe of. Anyway, timing led me to leave the park, cross the road, walk 50 yards, and cross another road in time to see a lady in tears walking towards me, holding a Christmas present bag, filled with pressies, pressing a tissue to her eye. I said something like:

'Don't worry, this time tomorrow it will be all over for another year'.

She shook her head at me, I have no idea what she thought I said, but she said something like:

'I am not having a good time; I have been stood up at a restaurant by my boyfriend'.

The woman had tears in her eyes as she explained she had been to a restaurant to meet her boyfriend (who she had been seeing for ten months) only to be stood up at the restaurant. Her boyfriend didn't show up. I stood and listened to the whole story of how this woman in her sixties who had been giving thousands of pounds to a man who has had a leg amputated because of his drug use, he let her down on her birthday, a couple of weeks before Christmas, and now on Christmas Day.

She showed me a gold bracelet he had given her, so he must be genuine, she thought. I told her there are more important things in life than money, and how he treats her is more important than the money he appears to spend on her. I was thinking he had probably used her money to buy the bracelet. Giving her gold doesn't prove anything.

She had spent the last twelve years on her own every Christmas, this was to be the first year which she spent with someone she thought cared about her. She had been looking forward to spending it with someone who cared. She said she had been angry with him, and she had told him not to treat her badly.

I tried to break through her righteous indignation, assuring her that she deserved better, and she had to treat herself better this year, because she can't change him and letting her down on her birthday and on Christmas Day is cruel.

Poor woman, to have moved to Southend from somewhere out of town and to have fallen prey to a typical Essex user, to the tune of thousands of pounds! I offered her a tissue No, she wasn't crying, she said. Dabbing her eyes, she just had a chill in her eye.

We said our goodbyes and I walked away thinking of our meeting. All the little things which had happened to delay my journey, to put me in the Right Place at the Right Time to be able to hear the woman's story. It did help her, to have me listen. It also helped me, to remind me that as a professional listener and counsellor, I am in the right role for my personality and skills. It helped me to be so grateful. I have learnt that lesson many years ago, I am so grateful to have learnt the importance of self-respect.

Having self-respect, a healthy respect for yourself is the best protection anyone can have from being used, abused, treated badly or cruelly. Thank you, God, the Universe, on Christmas Day 2017 for allowing me the experience of being of service and also being reminded that I could have easily been that other woman. There but for the grace of God that bought me to reading self-help books, which helped me to learn that it doesn't take a relationship to have a happy life.

The Happy feelings must be there while you are single, otherwise, what are you bringing to the relationship? You must know how to be happy in yourself first, before you head into relationships with other people.

I have also found that a lot of people believe that in order to have a happy life it involves having a relationship with another human, no matter what sort of low life they are, how little they think of you, this is the Holy Grail of Life. It is what is expected by people in Society, hopefully the younger generation are getting the message that a relationship is great, but not at any cost.

I realise it is a generalisation, but I think older women have been conditioned and brainwashed, pressured into finding a lifelong partner, preferably to marry, a myth perpetuated by men who have conditioned women to believe they are worthless if they are single and must have a relationship at all costs.

She was in her sixties the woman I spoke to, brought up in an era when women weren't listened to, often had little socio economic clout and although she has more money than the addict she hooked up with, she still has such low self-esteem as to believe the words a man says when he takes money from her, believing that he is genuine because she doesn't know what real love feels like.

I went home with a prayer for her and a prayer for myself and giving thanks to the Universe:

Thank you, Universe, for the seagulls who needed mince pies today. Thank you for the woman who stopped to have a chat with me in the street. Thank you for allowing me to listen.

Chapter V

Assigning Meanings

What follows, dear reader, is a list of items that can show up in your life and what it may mean.

Of course, any symbol can have whatever meaning you wish to give it. I am sharing with you here my understanding and experience of what shows up around the times of my own personal experience and the meanings I have learnt to give them.

Some meanings have been passed down through the generations, from my mum, her mum, and so on. Some of the meanings I have created myself because of my own life events. The meanings are very personal to each individual. Feel free to add your own meanings, keep your own journal and write down the symbols as and when they appear for you.

I would recommend interpreting your own messages. What is the Universe trying to tell you? I have included a list of symbols and their possible meanings; this isn't something which is intended to be used as a symbolic dictionary. It is there to show you some of the meanings which I can link with those symbols. You can link your own meanings. Write your own list of symbols in your diary, as they happen. Pay attention to what happens in your world in the following days and weeks.

The unfolding of life-changing events often takes a while, sometimes life-changing events happen suddenly, unexpected changes, but of course there are symbols for that! Whenever I see four crows, I know there are some huge changes coming up. It is significant enough for me to pay attention to. When four crows show up, I pay more attention to what is going on around me, right now, not at some time in the future. I know that Spirit is using those crows to get my attention.

The purpose of writing down the events of your life in a diary, is so that you can identify what the symbols mean for you. If you see two beautiful white birds land near you, you may appreciate that moment and thank the Universe/God/Higher Intelligence, and in a few days from that moment you may begin a new job which leads to a new friendship or a new relationship. Two white birds can now have meaning for you, next time you see a pair of white birds, you will know what you are likely to experience, or even remind you of a happier time in your life, which might lift your spirits.

The meanings of symbols and events is so individual to each of us, using my list of symbols to understand meanings would be a bit like using my astrological birth chart to understand your own life. There may be similarities in some of the symbols.

As with Carl Jung's archetypes of people in our consciousness, was his theory, and he is the grandfather of psychology, many people have accepted his ideas of how we function as humans in an attempt to understand ourselves and others.

So, feel free to read my list of symbols, but please know this is a very small, condensed version of the greater meanings and may bear no relation to your world, the meanings I have given to help with your understanding of what possibilities may exist, a prompt for your imagination and higher self to work on.

Another game that I like to play with the Universe is to 'assign' symbols to the people in my life. One of my friends is the Unicorn, whenever I see a Unicorn in the form of a picture or a toy in a shop or a print on soft furnishing, I take a photo of it and send it to her. Just to let her know the Universe is reminding me of her.

I have a friend who I associate with a white cat, because she is deaf, and white cats are often deaf. If I see a white cat, I message my friend, or I pay attention and often she will show up on my doorstep for an impromptu visit, or she will message me first. Try it for yourself, dear reader. Think of your loved ones and see what animal comes to mind when you think of them, or inanimate object if you prefer, and then test the Universe. See how often the Universe will put that item onto your path. It is a fun game and sometimes it can by so full of synchronicity and coincidence that it can take your breath away.

Here is my list for you, dear reader, my understanding of what these items mean when you see them on your path. Either literally, on your path, in your daily world, on your walk to work, your jogging route, your bus stop or as you pass by on the other side of the street. Even digitally, the figures and symbols show up on our google searches, almost as a sidebar to the thing we are searching for. One thing often leads to another, seemingly randomly.

Inanimate objects

Balloons: Something to celebrate, a reason to be cheerful.

Coats: There is always more than one layer, look deeper.

Coins: Money. Check your thoughts, feelings and beliefs about money. See a penny, pick it up and all day long you will have good luck!

Cuddly Toys: Whatever the animal, the symbolism is

the same, no matter whether it is a stuffed toy, a china toy, wicker work or knitted, it is the symbol which bears the meaning. Also, a symbol of something valuable which has been lost, a warning not to be careless with things or people you care about.

Dummies: Where are you being stupid? Are you being a dummy. Or do you need to keep quiet about something. Least said, soonest mended.

Forks: A decision to be made which can change your direction. A choice. Usually of two paths.

Four Leaf Clover: Generally seen as lucky. Good fortune to follow.

Gloves: Seeing Gloves can mean a few things. I had a message from a medium once who gave me a pair of gloves from Spirit, telling me that once the hard work is done, you can take the gloves off. You know, like gardening gloves, you might literally throw the gloves on the grass while you have a drink of water or cup of tea!

I take the Gloves as a sign to remember to relax and put myself in a state of relief, as if the work has been done. I am reminded of all the hard work I have done and to ease myself into the next steps, being aware that the hardest part is over. There is no need to make the next steps any more difficult than they need to be.

Of course, when people say 'the gloves are off' this can also reference a fight, taking the gloves off means the fighting is over. There is no need for any more fighting. Making peace with anyone or any situation which is troubling you and feeling like a fight.

It can also mean bare-knuckle fighting. Taking the gloves off, removing the padding so as to inflict more damage.

Hair Bow: Decoration, take a bow, enjoy feeling pretty and thank the Universe for the reminder.

Hairbrush: Brush it away, whatever tangles you are dealing with, there is always a way to soothe it out, or smooth it out.

Hair Grip: Sometimes used for picking locks. Is there something in your world which needs unpicking? Or is there something that you are gripping too tightly? Is there something that you need to get to grips with?

Hats: Hats Off to you from the Universe. A little nod from Spirit that you have done a good job, and achieved a recent goal. Also, a sign for needing a new hat, can be a sign of attendance at a wedding. A hat can also mean that you have a new role to play in life. Choose a new hat. Choose a new role.

Hearse: Horse drawn hearse. Sign of news of a death. The horse doesn't necessarily have to be drawing a coffin behind it. Just the horse without a coffin is enough.

Hearse: Not the horse drawn version, does symbolize

death. It is superstition to hold a button until you see an animal or a bird. This is supposed to be good luck and help to hold off your own demise.

Horseshoe: Holds the luck inside. If the horseshoe is turned upside down, all the luck falls out.

Jackets: Some things need covering up, check under the cover, do you need a protective layer.

Keys: New doors opening, expect to be handed a new key, either to your own door or someone else's door. Keys are extremely symbolic of new openings, unlocking new levels of understanding and areas which were previously locked to us.

Lighters: Living a lighter life, let go of anything which no longer serves you. Check if you are carrying unwanted thoughts, such as worry, or needless emotion such as guilt or feeling responsible for something which isn't your fault or is in the past, are you carrying too much weight than is good for you, would you feel better if you were literally living a lighter life?

Magpies: One for sorrow, two for joy, three for a girl and four for a boy, five for silver, six for gold, seven for a secret never to be told.

Money: I prefer to see coins as a gift from the Universe. A little prod from Spirit to remind you to follow the money, and pay attention to where a new avenue or door may open for you which will lead to an improved financial situation.

Wayne Dyer gave talks when he was alive, some of his talks are available for free on YouTube. He tells a story of how he thanked the Universe every time he saw a coin, and he picked it up, grateful for his find, he took the coins home and collected them in a jar, for years. It wasn't until he was in much later life that he asked his assistant to give them away to charity after he had been diagnosed with illness and was moving home. He had over £3,000 dollars in coins.

It wasn't about the value of the money, it was the idea of abundance, of knowing that money is flowing to us and through us, money is available to us, as long as we can stay in tune with the Universal energies of the providing universe and not shut ourselves off from the flow of abundance.

Pants: Liar, liar, pants on fire. Check where you are lying to yourself or others. Americans use this word to also mean trousers. British people call underwear, pants. To see a pair of pants on your path may seem like an odd experience, and maybe your life is about to take a turn for the unbelievable, the surreal. Or do you need to pull your pants up? Is there something in your life you could be doing better?

Pens: Who do you need to write to? A relative? An employer, a legal situation which needs you to write something? Are you a writer and Spirit is asking you to put pen to paper, write a book, blog, and reach out to others on social media? Whatever you need to write, start now.

Phones: Expect a phone call. A reminder to call someone. Is it time to call someone? A symbol for communication. Is there someone you need to communicate with?

Scarves: Warmth around the throat and voice, speak with warm, kind, loving words.

Shorts: About to be pulled up short. Are you taking a short cut?

Shirts: Dressing up for an event. Is someone being shirty with you? Are you being shirty with someone else?

Shoes: New shoes to walk in. Never judge another until you have walked two full moons in their moccasins.

Socks: Put a sock in it! Listen more, speak less.

Stopped Clocks: This is really a mystery of life. I do love to see stopped clocks. Time is one of the most mysterious elements of life and can mean so many different things to different people. A reminder that time isn't actually as linear as we imagine it to be. Time waits for no man. Life is too short to wait. Time to take stock of your current situation. Time to...insert your own goal here.

Trainers: There will be some training to do, physical, mental, emotional, or maybe a life lesson is about to happen. You are about to be schooled. Or you could be the trainer. Eyes open for a student who may benefit from your knowledge. When the Master is ready, the student appears. Or as one of my friends happily pointed out, the Universe is saying there is a situation that needs running away from, it is 'Time to jog on'! #lol.

Trousers: Who is in charge of your life? A reminder that you wear the trousers. Ask yourself how you feel about control? Do you have enough control, do you try and control others, is someone else trying to control you?

Windmills: The winds of change doth blow, time for change. Remember, whatever it is, this too will pass.

Colours

The different colours are extremely important and personal to each individual. For instance, if someone had a recently deceased loved one who had a purple funeral, purple flowers, purple balloons, and they asked everyone to wear purple and as they were thinking of them, a shop which specialised in purple showed up on their path, it would have significant meaning for that person.

It is also possible to see coloured auras surrounding people. I find it particularly easy to see the auras of psychic mediums when they are working on platforms in spiritualist churches. The communication from Spirit looks like a big cloud of coloured smoke, you know how it looks when people Vape and a giant cloud wafts away from them? That is what communication from Spirit looks like when you can tune in to the visual manifestation.

I also wonder if the colours we wear are instrumental in helping to attract what we want into our lives. Wearing black often acts as protection from the outside world and just absorbs all the vibes which come our way. White, therefore, it would seem obvious to me, would reflect what comes to us. Probably wanted as well as unwanted. Which is great if you want to be a shining beacon of light to everyone around you.

The general meanings of the different colours are as follows:

Black: The absence of colour. For protection, privacy, sensitivity and secrecy, mourning, serious, definitive also the unknown, the hidden.

Blue: Healing, traditional, calm, peace, love and freedom. Can also symbolise a cool feeling. Are you being too cool with someone? Or not cool enough? Check your emotional temperature.

Green: Nature, peace, serenity, the heart chakra. Green can also be a sign to watch out for envy and jealousy, either from you to others or from others to you.

Orange: Warmth, harmony, growth, success, love,

embracing everyone. Are you feeling included? Is anyone feeling left out?

Pink: Romance, kindness, generosity, love, friendship, feelings of warmth and security. Sign of good health.

Purple: High-minded intellect, connection to source, spirit, religion, higher self.

Red: Power, masculine energy, fiery, dynamic, passion. Also a symbol of danger. Time to keep your senses on full alert.

White: Purity, encompasses all colours, neutral, spiritual, powerful.

Yellow: Intuition, intelligence, positivity, happiness. Also, watch out for someone using a fake smile to mask sadness or ill-health.

Rainbow: 'Hello' from Spirit, a nod from a recently deceased person, Universal Love.

Animals and Birds

Land animals, water creatures and beings who fly. The three categories of animal types bring with them many different messages. All animals are directly connected to source and tend not to cut themselves off or cause themselves suffering or pain, in the same way that humans are able to. Unless you find a particularly neurotic cat or horse, and even then, they have only become that way because of the time they have spent with humans.

Creatures of the air are associated with matters of higher knowledge, and often guide us, or try to, towards higher learning and greater self-awareness.

Land animals are intuitive, grounded and stable both mentally and physically. Whenever we are blessed with a visit from a land animal it is because our own vibration is in harmony with theirs and they are happy to be around us.

Water creatures are symbolic of all things spiritual and water is the element which governs emotions. To have an encounter with a creature of the sea usually leaves a person feeling privileged.

Reptiles and insects are symbols of fortitude, resilience, ambition and strength.

Bird in the house: sign of a coming death

Blackbirds: Friends, making a new friend, hearing from an old friend.

Black cats: A clear sign of good luck and good fortune about to cross your path. Many people, particularly in the United States of America, see the black cat as being a sign of bad luck, many people in the United Kingdom do love to see a black cat and see it as a sign of luck.

They are often ignored and because of their colour,

they can go about their daily business pretty much unnoticed. If you heighten your awareness, observation and spirituality, you will notice whenever a black cat shows up for you.

Butterflies: Catalyst, freedom, change, personal growth, spiritual growth, happiness.

Bird Poo: Traditionally this is meant to be a lucky sign. Good luck is about to befall you. I think of it as someone in Spirit trying to get your attention and using a bird to do it. That is the best way for the bird that he could think of! What else was he supposed to do?

Crab: Security comes from within, pay attention to any harshness, either cynicism or mistrust of other people. Practicalities around housing, moving house.

Dead Bird: Sign of an impending passing. Death of a project or expectation.

A single Crow/Raven: News from spirit, news on earth, something to crow about, can mean news of a death.

A pair of Crows/Ravens: Good news.

Three Crows/Ravens: Good news involving a family member.

Four Crows/Ravens: Huge change, a move, an unexpected disruption.

Dogs: Loyalty, friendship. A new friend is on the

horizon. Pay attention to your friends, is there someone who is in need of extra help now?

Dolphin: Dolphins are often considered to be highly intelligent, sensitive creatures. If one shows up on your path, consider yourself honoured and blessed.

Dragonfly: A symbol of spiritual growth, huge change ahead and a portent of personal upheaval resulting in extreme personal development.

Eagle: Strength, freedom.

Elephant: Carrying a heavy load, loyal, reliable person, slow action, there's no rush to do anything at this moment in time, for you, right now. Take stock of your life and people. Make sure you are only carrying your load and not baggage other people have given you.

Feathers: Angels are around you now, blessings are upon you. A reminder to treat other people as kindly as you can.

Flock of Birds: Marriage, news of a wedding, invite to a wedding.

Foxes: Family, resources, check all your family members are okay. Watch out for sneaky, underhand, unexpected behaviour or an untrustworthy person on the horizon.

Ginger Cats: Spirit, friends in spirit, anyone recently

deceased.

Giraffe: Harmony, peace, kindness, gentleness, Do you need to wind your neck in or are you being asked to stick your neck out?

Goat: Reliable, hardworking, cleanliness, bossy, hard headed. The symbol represents Capricorn, the sea goat. If you see a goat show up in your world, have a look at if you have a Capricorn born person in your world, check whether they need your help in any way, or reach out and contact them. People born under this sign are notoriously bad at asking for or accepting help.

Horses: Strength, freedom, power, growth, speed, travel. Movement.

Jackal: Living on your wits.

Lion: The King or Queen of the jungle, love, warm-hearted, passion, strength, courage, leadership, someone born under the sign of Leo.

Meerkat: Support of a group, being part of a group, keeping an eye open.

Ostrich: Sticking your head in the sand, oblivious to the truth, denying the truth, not seeing what or who is in front of you.

Pigeon: Looking in the wrong place for abundance or love, pecking at crumbs, catching crumbs off someone else's plate. Reach for your own source of sustenance.

Poo of any description: Nothing good can come of this. Unless you really appreciate the poop to value ratio. You can't make a pancake without breaking some eggs, right? You can't have the smooth without the rough. Poo is a sign of a rough patch.

Ram: Hard-headed, Aries-like, fiery, dynamic, leading the way, headstrong, capable, speedy. If you are fortunate enough to have a person in your life who is born under the sun sign of Aries, seeing a ram, either a real ram or a picture of one, or a stuffed toy, is a reminder from the Universe of that person. What you do with that message is up to you, contact them, check up on them, reach out, text, call, email. Or you can just wait and see if they show up in your world.

Robins: Spirit messengers, a reminder from a loved one in spirit.

Seagulls: Independence, strength, freedom, exploring new areas.

Squirrel: High energy, action, saving money, no matter how small, review money, protect your resources, speedy action.

Stag: The Stag is often a symbol for a mature, powerful male. The symbol for coming of age and leadership. The stag often represents a person in your world.

Tortoiseshell cat: Friends, new opportunities, seek new paths, accept and love the diversity of life.

White cats: Deaf people; lighten up; spiritual power coming your way; are you turning a deaf ear to someone or something in your life?

Zebra: Friends, gentle power, power of the vegetarian animal, gentle loving strength.

Signs in Nature

Crescent moon: New beginning, fresh start, time to drop unwanted habits, there is a direct line for you to Spirit, you are able to communicate directly with your higher self.

Flowers: Personal meaning, a reminder of beauty, miracles, depending on the flower, they each have their own meaning, books have been written on this subject alone, and I take them as gifts from Spirit.

Often spirit messages are ended with a symbolic flower being given to the person who is having the reading. A reminder of the temporary experience of life. Red Roses symbolise love and are often used as a symbol to show love from Spirit.

Full moon: Love everyone you meet, unconditional love, loving emotional connection, appreciate the feminine.

Star: Direction, check you are heading in the direction you want to be travelling, every thought, feeling and action is taking you either away from your goal or closer to your destination. You are made of the same stuff of stars. We are all stars.

Trees: Life, branches of a tree, family, relationships, growth, secure your own roots.

Urine: Is someone taking the mickey out of you? As in, literally taking the pee!

Water: Associated with emotions, leaks, be aware of where you could be at risk of leaking over other people, or inappropriate emotional attachment.

Mythical creatures

Phoenix: re-birth, rising from the ashes, a comeback.

Dragon: power, passion, fierce strength at your disposal, enchant the dragon.

Water serpent: emotional power, engage with the undercurrents, uncover hidden depths.

Centaur: Masculine power.

Unicorn: You are asking for the non-existent, a miracle which seems impossible, miracles rarely happen instantly, look at where you are hoping for something that cannot happen by itself, what can you do to make this miracle happen?

Life Events

Being asked for change: Yes, you have an opportunity to be the person who gives, or not, your choice, but also to be prepared for change in your own life.

Being asked for Directions: remember you are the person who knows the Way.

Being asked for a light: Remember the light you can bring to situations and people. Time to lighten up.

Being asked for a pen: Is there something you need to write? A prompt from the Universe to pick up a pen and start writing.

Being asked for help: A reminder from the Universe that you are in the right place at the right time to be of service. You have been trusted to be the person who is able to help.

Being called the wrong name: Do you know anyone who is called that name? You are being reminded of them. Whether you contact them is up to you, but the Universe is bringing you a reminder of them for a reason.

Being mistaken for someone else: how easy it is to be there for others. You are being used as a cooperative component, as a reminder for someone else. What is the name of the person you are being mistaken for? Do you know someone with that name?

Bumping into someone you know: A reminder of Universal Intelligence.

Cars giving way: The Universe is a giving place, full of helpful companions.

Finding Lost Pets: You are the rescuer; spirit is using you to be able to help others.

People thinking, they know you: Which is not the same as being mistaken for someone else! When people look at you and try and place you, as if they know you from somewhere but can't remember where. Again, a reminder of Spirit, there is more going on that we can see.

Sneezing: Okay, maybe not a life 'event', but I didn't really know where else to put it. There is a little rhyme that goes along with sneezing:

Once a wish, twice a kiss, three's a letter and four is something better.

A family pet sneezing, or two people sneezing at the same time is also a sign of good luck.

Numbers

All the numbers have meaning. There is no doubt about that. If you have a look on Amazon I am pretty sure that you could find a book written about each of these numbers. I have mentioned it earlier in this book, the numbers 3,6 and 9 being given extra meaning by Nikola Tesla. I wonder how long it will be before AI uncovers the mystery of the universe and the role of numbers.

Number Zero: Your situation has gone full circle. You are at one with a Universe made of Ones and Zeros. You have a plateau ahead before the next period of growth begins. A stable place to spend some time to contemplate your most recent life journey. Call to patience before the call to action.

Number One: Wholeness, unity, self, ambition, force.

Number Two: Struggle, opposites, opposing forces, balance.

Number Three: God, the Trinity, Spirituality, one plus two equals birthing of true wisdom.

Number Four: Harmony, balance, solid foundation.

Number Five: Masculine energy, full on, dynamic, family.

Number Six: Feminine energy, intuition, harmony, growth and abundance.

Number Seven: Completion of Cycles, Sun. Good luck, seven planets, seven Roman Gods, Hinduism believes in seven major chakras, Arabs have seven holy temples, Japan has seven lucky Gods, and there are seven ancient Buddhas.

In the Bible, God created the Universe in seven days. King Solomon took seven years to build a temple. In the Torah, seven years is one holy year; the dead are mourned for seven days. Revelation has seven seals, there are seven sacraments, seven stars, seven deadly sins, seven plagues of heavenly virtues, seven winning on a game of craps, 3 x 7 wins at Blackjack, both sides of a dice add up to seven. Breaking a mirror brings seven years bad luck (in many cultures, the mirror is seen as a symbol of the reflection of the soul). 7 Wonders of the World, 7 seas, 7 continents, 7 notes of music, 7 colours of the rainbow, 7 spots on a ladybird. In China the 7 represents Death.

Number Eight: Infinity, eternity.

Number Nine: Birth, new life, nine pregnant months.

Number 10: Masculine energy, power, acquiring, sudden unexpected good news.

Number 11 or 11:11: You are going through a change in your life, your personal development and spiritual awareness has begun. Knock, knock. The Universe is knocking on the fabric of your life. You are being invited to be a lightworker, a healer, a Way Shower, the person who Knows the Way.

One of those people who 'know' the right thing to do, which doesn't include analytical thought. Intuition is strong. Psychic abilities are about to increase and hone up.

Feeling at One with the Planet, the Universe, your own little community. Wherever you go, the place you are in will improve because of your presence.

This can also be a calling for you to figure out your specific purpose, the calling in your life, you will be influencing other people, not by who you are, but by how you are. You are a Human Being, not a Human Doing.

You will Know your Purpose. Your Soul Purpose is about to be revealed to you.

The synchronicities will begin. Clues as to what is going on. Examples of what is going on for you will materialize into your physical reality.

A sign that you are in harmony and synchronized with the universe for your path, you are on the right path, the right track, the right direction.

There is about to be positive change which may feel dreadful in the short term, such as being fired from your job or made redundant which in the long run turns out to be the perfect turning point for your life.

Number 12: The Goddess, feminine energy, cosmic order, feeling.

Number 13: Unlucky for some, Friday 13th, Lucky for Others. There is a lot of history surrounding the number 13. Chinese and ancient Egyptians believed that it brings good fortune. Egyptians believed there were 12 stages of life toward spiritual enlightenment, and the 13th stage was the eternal afterlife.

The negative belief about 13 was because Judas was the 13th person to be seated at the Last Supper with Jesus Christ.

Number 18: Wayne Dyer shares his stories of where this number shows up for him. One and eight, meaning the One Infinite Source. He noticed when 18 showed up, and even 81. In his story he mentioned noticing the Bhagavad Gita having 18 chapters and the Tao Te Ching has 81 chapters.

Number 22: In Kabbalah, the number 22 is significant as it responds to the total number of letters in the Hebrew alphabet. Each Hebrew letter in the alphabet is attributed with symbolic and mystical meanings within the Kabbalistic tradition.

In the Kabbalistic system known as the Tree of Life, the Hebrew letters are associated with specific paths or sephiroth (emanations of divine energy). The paths connect the sephiroth on the tree and represent different spiritual aspects and qualities.

Number 23: A common number to show up. Every number has the capacity to symbolise meaning, of course. This number 23 was chosen for the film that Jim Carey starred in (mentioned elsewhere in the book). The number 23 can also be significant as a reminder of a person who passed at the age of 23.

Number 27: There is a well-known 27 club. Unfortunately, the 27 club consists of celebrities who all died at the age of 27. Equally, there is probably a 21 club, or 22 club and a club for every age that a loved one was, when they passed over.

Number 33: Help from Jesus, Holy Spirit. A call for you to spend some time in meditation. Find a space for appreciation, every day. This is not the same as gratitude, to feel appreciation is a form of meditation and spiritual practice.

Number 47: Something going on around working for money. More work will be coming your way, more opportunities. Take a look for the gold amongst the dirt. There is always a way to find the golden nuggets even in the dirtiest of situations. Where there is muck, there is brass.

Number 111: Triples of any digit are all significant. Think positive thoughts which bring happiness and hope. The more you think of something, the more it shows up for you.

Number 137: The mathematical enigma. Pray, speak to the Universe. Acknowledge that you have seen this number for a reason. Is there something you need to do or something you need to stop doing? Stop in your tracks and re-assess your current path.

Number 222: Part of the pathway, often follows on from 111. New ideas are growing into reality, keep watering them, like watering a seed in the ground. Just because you can't see the seed preparing to sprout through the earth, doesn't mean that your watering isn't helping.

Use your thoughts like water. Don't quit five minutes before the miracle of manifestation appears. Keep affirming and visualizing. Don't Give Up. Never Give Up (and don't get caught).

Number 251: Encouragement. Keep going.

Number 313: The time-of-day Wayne Dyer used to wake up. Are you waking up at the same time every day?

Number 320: Deaths often occur at 3.20 am. I have no idea why this happens, but ask any nurse or doctor who has worked on a nightshift, and they will tell you there is a 'witching hour', and the most common time for people to die, is between the hour of 3 am – 4 am.

Number 321: Counting down to lift off! Time is nearly here to experience whatever it is that you have been expecting.

Number 333: The trilogy. A highly spiritual number. Lift your inner self up to being as spiritual as you can. Clean living, clean thinking, clean eating. Live your life as if something amazing is about to happen. Be ready.

Number 444: Angels, when triple four shows up,

Guardian Angels are near, reassuring you that All is Well. Remind yourself, regularly, All is Well. If in doubt, make this your hourly mantra.

Number 555: Life changes are upon you, neither Good nor Bad, life is a natural flow within which there are always changes.

Some changes appear unwanted but turn out to be the best thing that has ever happened to us, some changes appear good on the surface, but later down the road, turn into a terrible life event we barely noticed.

The Universe does have a propensity towards chaos, so why are we so surprised about change? Humans generally don't seem to like change and yet they also crave interest. Check your own fears about change.

Number 666: Not the number of the devil, but the number of financial abundances. Are your thoughts out of balance? Materialism, abundance and harmony. Check your feelings about God and the Universe. As Albert Einstein is credited with saying 'The most important decision that we have to make is whether we believe we live in a friendly, or hostile, Universe'.

Number 777: A fabulous completion of work done, time for a breather. Angels applaud you. Your wish is on its way, expect miracles to occur. Completion.

Number 888: Eternity, there is no past present or future, the only time is now. Time to prepare, winding up an emotional phase. Crops are ripe, enjoy them now, enjoy the fruits of your labour.

Number 999: Birth, re-birth, new beginnings. Completion for lightworkers, healing, reiki practitioners, get to work, mother earth needs you. Preaching to others. Or as some people call it 'spreading the Word'.

In China, the number 999 is considered highly auspicious, three lots of three equals nine and three lots of that!

Randomly throwing in a number that is auspicious in China, reminds me that every number is probably seen as highly auspicious in some country somewhere. A reminder for you, dear reader, to interpret your own numbers.

Shapes

Triangle: Gender, inverted triangle for female, lunar, cave, passive, mother, erect triangle for male, solar, mountain, assertive, father.

Spiral: Often occurs in nature, the double helix of a DNA, and can be as large as a galaxy. The image of a spiral has been found decorated on an object in the Ukraine, 10,000 BCE. (Wikipedia).

There are many different types of Spirals, the Fibonacci Spiral, and the Golden Spiral to name just two. The spiral does have a few definitions, depending on whether you ask a mathematician or a scientist, and whether it is a 2d or 3d version. The spiral is created by a curve, emanating from a point, moving farther away as it circles the point.

For me, when I see a spiral, I am reminded that our lives often move in spirals. It is the journey of our life which often feels circular, we sometimes end up back where we started, but really, there has always been progress.

So, for me a spiral asks me to look at what I learned last time I was here, in this position. Am I going round in circles, or have I actually made any progress since I was last here?

Circle: Wholeness, completeness, eternity, never-ending, harmony. Otherwise, a symbol of going round in circles. It is time to take a step in a straight line, in a forward direction.

Five-pointed Star: The Pentagram or sometimes called the Golden Star, a symbol of mystical and magical significance.

Six-pointed Star: The Hexagram shows up in many of the world's religions. For further reading a good place to start would be Wikipedia. The hexagram has been used by various religions for everything from attaining nirvana to warding off illness and diseases.

Square: Four-sided, straight-lined, straightforward

shape. The Square is used by the Freemasons, who place great importance on the symbology of shapes and what they represent.

The Square is symbolic of a level man, morality and obeying the law of Truth. To see a square shape in your life can mean whatever a square means to you. Is it a box? A feeling of being boxed in. Do you need to think outside of the box or is there any area where you are convincing yourself you do not need to colour between the lines, and you are stretching the truth to suit your own ends?

Cube: The temple of God. The golden cube, the black cube, the diamond cube, the cube of curiosity. The Rubik cube. Is there a puzzle which is about to be solved? The use of higher intelligence to solve a practical problem.

Octagon: Whenever I see the eight of anything show up, I think of the sign for infinity. Some things are eternal. Or unsolvable, or beyond human comprehension. If the Octagon shows up for you, have a little twirl in the centre and hand your current problem over to the Universe. It might seem as if there is no way out, but there could be a way through.

Crescent: New Start. New beginnings.

Meaning of Sayings and Proverbs

'Bob's Your Uncle and Fanny's Your Aunt':

'Bob's your uncle' is an exclamation that is used when 'everything is alright' and the simple means of obtaining the successful result is explained.

For example, "left over right; right over left, and Bob's your uncle - a reef knot" or "she slipped the officer £100 and, Bob's your uncle', she was off the charge". (Courtesy of the Phrase Finder).

The Phrase Finder does offer three alternative origins and times when this phrase has been claimed, firstly surrounding nepotism in political appointments:

Bob's your uncle' is often said to derive from the supposed nepotism of Lord Salisbury, who appointed a favourite nephew, Arthur Balfour, to several political posts in the 1880s. Balfour went on to become Prime Minister after his uncle, but his early political appointments were considered inappropriate as he had shown no prior interest in public work.

A second interpretation has it that the phrase derives from the slang term 'all is bob', meaning 'all is well'. That term is listed in Captain Francis Grose's *Dictionary of the Vulgar Tongue,* 1785:

A shoplifter's assistant, or one that receives and carries off stolen goods. All is bob; all is safe.

The slang word 'bob', meaning 'shoplifter's assistant', had been in circulation for some years at that time and is defined as such in Nathan Bailey's *Dictionary of Canting and Thieving Slang*, 1721. More generally, 'bob' was used as a generic name for 'person', like 'Jack', 'Jill', 'Joe' etc. For example, public schoolboys who indulged in land sports like cricket or rugby were called 'dry bobs' and those who preferred boating were called 'wet bobs'.

The third potential source is the music hall. The earliest known example of the phrase in print is in the bill for a performance of a musical revue in Dundee called *Bob's Your Uncle*, which appeared in the Scottish newspaper *The Angus Evening Telegraph* in June 1924.

The expression also formed part of the lyrics of a song written by John P. Long and published in 1931 - *Follow Your Uncle Bob*. The lyrics include:

Bob's your uncle
Follow your Uncle Bob
He knows what to do
He'll look after you.

The difficulty with the first two suggested origins is the date. The phrase itself isn't recorded until the

1920. It would seem odd for a phrase to be coined about the nepotism of an uncle for his nephew well after both Prime Ministers were out of office. The 'all is bob' origin is from a century or so earlier and appears to have little reason to be connected to 'Bob's your uncle' other than that they both contain the word 'bob'.

This isn't the first time that an etymological outsider romps home when the favourites have fallen at the first fence. We don't know for sure but, based on current knowledge, this classically English expression may well prove to be Scottish and derive not from 10 Downing Street, but from the King's Theatre, Dundee.

'See a Penny pick it up and all day long you will have good luck':

"The origins of this superstition may stem from ancient times when metals were believed to offer protection from evil and harmful spirits to those who possessed them. When cultures started using coins as currency, obviously those who had more of them were considered wealthy." (www.psychiclibrary.com).

The origins are uncertain, but this began as superstition. Some people believing a Heads-Up penny is a sign of good luck, something to be celebrated, enjoyed and freely picked up, with a Tails Up penny to be avoided, left alone, because it will bring bad luck.

Other people believe the penny should be passed on to someone else, the same day, in order to ensure your own good luck. Another penny ritual is to put a penny into a bride's shoe, to ensure a happy and prosperous marriage. Putting a penny into a new handbag or purse is also a superstition believed to ensure a steady flow of cash.

MY FINAL COINCIDENCE STORY

Well, dear reader, you have made it to my final story of the year, which took place in 2023. The event in my life that I interpreted to mean that it is time to publish this book.

Are you sitting comfortably? Good, then I'll begin…May 2023, my little weekend trip to Amsterdam from the UK. I was attending a two-day extravaganza to go and see Esther Hicks in person. It was a beautiful experience and I loved it. I loved the hotel I stayed in, the night before flying, it was an unexpected hotel stay, due to an unexpected train strike.

I loved bumping into people who asked me for directions and yet who consequently ended up showing me the way instead!

I enjoyed the demonstration with Esther Hicks on the first day. I had dinner with newly found restaurant companions and when I went back up to my hotel room, I had not had any reason to open the curtains because it was late at night, or because I was tired, or because I just didn't think to. For whatever reason, the curtains were still closed when I went to bed.

The following morning, after a good night's sleep, I realized that I hadn't looked out at the view. I opened the curtains, and I was treated to a view of a green blanket of treetops. I was on the sixth floor and the hotel was in the middle of a seemingly quiet area. As I appreciated how green the trees were, I noticed a sign, bang in the middle of greenery.

A big red sign with giant red letters across it. It had a name on it. The name? Do I need to tell you, dear reader? 'BOB'.

I loved this coincidence. I sent up a thought:

'Thanks Bob, for the sign from Spirit'

I saw it, I paid attention, and publishing this book is the result.

Lots of love to you Bob and I will see you in the afterlife when I get there.

Tamasin x

p.s. dear reader, for those of you who are reading this book for the coincidence stories, this is the part where we part ways. The next chapter is an afterthought about all the other Woo that shows up.

Chapter VI

Curiouser and Curiouser
Otherwise known as Full Woo

'The Universe is not only stranger than we imagine, it is stranger than we imagine'.

Albert Einstein

I couldn't really have put this book together without at least mentioning the other weird and wonderful subjects which sometimes brush with synchronicity. The internet is full of strange stories. Theories about what we are doing on the planet and how long we have been here, conspiracy theories about Ancient Aliens and an Elite group of people who are secretly running the global economy.

There are so many rabbit holes involving supernatural claims which gain a lot of attention. Some of the subjects I am aware of, but they don't grab my interest enough for me to include them in this book, things like, demonic possession, exorcism, experimenting with Ouija boards.

All the subjects covered regularly by Art Bell in his Coast to Coast radio show, things like, UFOs, alien abductions, hidden cave dwellers, reptilian shapeshifters, mothman, the black-eyed children and the Men in Black and probably many more unexplained urban myths that are too numerous to mention in this space.

A lot of these conspiracies are talked about and written about by people like David Icke, who seems to be de-platformed so often that it just adds to the conspiracy narrative.

I can't take a lot of what he talks about seriously, but I do admire the courage of his conviction. I think he lost me on the reptilian shapeshifters. But who knows?

Maybe some of these things are only evident in some of our lives. That has to be a possibility. Since there appear to be infinite possibilities, why wouldn't that be an option?

Another area that I haven't really mentioned much in this book is tarot reading, clairvoyance, communicating with the afterlife, with our eyes open. Not in a sleep state, not half-asleep, or dreaming, but wide awake. You know, seeing the spirit of a dead person appear in front of us. Again, I think that could be worthy of a book all by itself.

Near Death Experiences (NDEs)

However, the subject of NDEs is a different matter. Near Death Experiences are when a person dies, physically, they are technically dead, for whatever reason, and yet they are still aware of themselves.

If you look on Youtube, there are some people talking about NDEs, they are often stories where people have narrowly missed death. These people seem to be unaware that the term 'Near Death Experience' has been coined by Raymond Moody to cover the experience of actually dying and coming back to life.

Raymond Moody opened the dialogue around this subject in his book after life after death in the '70s, which was an amazing feat, pre-internet (R.A. Moody,1975) Life After Life the book was called, and is now available instantly on Kindle! His book is full of people sharing their NDEs and I would recommend anyone to have a read of it.

When Dr. Raymond Moody compiled these stories, he managed to find some common threads amongst them, not all of them, but a lot of people, having died, found themselves in a tunnel, heading towards a bright light. When they passed through the tunnel, they were met by loved ones, people who had already passed over. Some people had conversations or were given the choice to come back, some people were told they had to come back because it wasn't their time.

Anyway, it is a fascinating read and I feel it is as close as we can get to 'evidence' that there is more to life than what we can see going on around us in our daily lives.

There are also channels on Youtube where people share their Near Death Experiences. People die. Technically dead. They go to some sort of heaven, that often involves a 'life review', they look back over times in their lives when they have been kind to people, times when they have been unkind to people, all of it.

Then they come back, often revived with a desire to let everyone know about their experience. I am guessing there are also people who have had these experiences that they don't want to share with everyone.

The only story I haven't heard from a Near Death Experience is the one where Guardian Angels talk a person through how they could have used the Law of Attraction better to make more money. Strangely, the subject of money seems to be missing from many of these stories. Maybe the NDE'ers aren't allowed to remember all of their experience? I have heard stories where the person is told by their Guardian Angel/Spirit Guide/Loved one in Spirit, that they aren't going to remember everything that they are being told,

The Law of Attraction

The frequencies we give out as human beings is like a radio transmitter which will propel you into the lighter, faster frequencies. A little quote from Esther Hicks:

'We are all vibrational beings. You're like a receiving mechanism that when you set your tuner to the station, you're going to hear what's playing. Whatever you are focused upon is the way you set your tuner, and when you focus there for as little as 17 seconds, you activate that vibrations within you. Once you activate a vibration within you, Law of Attraction beings responding to that vibration, and you're off and running – whether it's something wanted or unwanted'.

Excerpted from North Los Angeles, CA – Sunday August 18th 2002

This is the idea of the Law of Attraction. This is probably a good time to mention Nikola Tesla again. Nikola Tesla believed that the fundamental nature of the Universe is based on energy, frequency and vibration. He stated 'If you want to find the secrets of the Universe, think in terms of energy, frequency and vibration'. According to him, everything in the Universe, including physical objects and even our thoughts, emit energy and has its unique frequency and vibration.

Tesla recognised the significance of frequency in the transmission and utilisation of electrical energy. He conducted numerous experiments and developed devices based on the principles of resonance and oscillation. One of his most famous inventions is the Tesla coil, which uses resonant circuits to generate high-frequency electrical currents and wireless transmission of power.

Of course, it is possible that a mind that can come up with the idea of x-rays (even though he wasn't the person who eventually succeeded in making an x-ray machine, his mind was on the wavelength of the thoughts and ideas that would go on to create the x-ray machine), is also capable of becoming obsessed with the number 3? Yes, I guess it is possible. He must have had his reasons, maybe he wasn't in touch with his feelings? He probably wouldn't have been would he?

At that time, men generally weren't encouraged to even acknowledge their feelings, let alone place any importance on them. It is possible that Nikola Tesla was trying to hoover his carpet without plugging the hoover into the socket (as Esther Hicks says). If you aren't lined up with Source before you take action, you might as well be trying to make toast in a toaster that isn't plugged in.

Taking the path of least resistance may not, at first glance, appear to be the desirable or 'wanted' path, or the ideal circumstances, but the path of least resistance will lead you at least a step closer towards what you do want. The Universe is an absolute, complete, just, practical, exacting reflection of the energy we are giving out.

If what shows up on the outside is not acceptable to you, or is undesirable, or unwanted, then at least you are being shown how you are thinking and feeling. You have the power to adjust your own thoughts, thereby generating new feelings.

You have the power to create your own reality. By fully acknowledging that you are the author of your own life. With a capital L. Your Life. Your choices. You have the power to create a desired future. You have unlimited potential, you can decide, and watch, as the Universe conspires to make it happen, offering you guidance in the form of synchronicity and coincidence along the way.

The reason I include the Law of Attraction in the Woo section is because a lot of people don't believe in it. I love the Law of Attraction, and I would love to believe that we have a point of attraction that the Universe is responding to. If you can't believe the idea that you are a magnet, try it. Try exploring how you feel and see what shows up.

The next step is to try and suspend disbelief and accept that whatever showed up was in response to how you were feeling! I know, it is a stretch, which is why it is in the Woo section. Give it a go, try it, what have you got to lose? Or rather, what have you got to gain? If all that happens is that you feel better, then why not give it a go?

Since we all have the power to create, there is nothing stopping us from starting right now. Attract whatever you want, ideas, circumstances, people and opportunities. All you have to do is to feel your way towards the feeling as if you already have whatever it is that you want.

When the signs and coincidences begin to show up, which they will, you must decide to take action. The guidance which shows up on the outside, is a direct mirror of what you are offering from the inside.

The Mandela Effect

So, dear reader, a short trip into the Mandela Effect. Not everyone will have heard of the Mandela Effect, so, bear with me while I try and find a little explanation. The Mandela Effect. What is it? Well, for me, the coincidences are communication from The Universe, from God, from Spirit, our Guardian Angels, our Higher Selves. It is quite mystical and not entirely easy to explain.

I am working from the assumption that there is a Higher Intelligence at work. In the Universe. Which is all well and good, until scientists, physicists, mathematicians and anyone with an interest in the reality of the earth and its origins, throw in the evidence that actually, we do not live in just a Universe.

We live in multi-verses. Parallel Universes, more than one Universe, with every possible eventuality and every possible likelihood being carried out to its conclusion. Since scientists are not even claiming to have all the answers, I cannot possibly claim to have any idea of how our little consciousness and our daily decision making has any sort of bearing on producing a whole new reality. Who knows which events change a sequence of events? How serious, or how important or how big a decision has to be before it does have a knock-on effect on surrounding decisions and life choices.

Is it really EVERY decision that we make? Can that even be possible? For our little minds it can be quite mind-boggling to contemplate that particular theory. But for us humans, with our restricted intelligence, and I mean that in the nicest possible way, even the most intelligent amongst us would struggle to remember more than one set of memories at a time, surely?

It can be a big ask to get our heads around even the possibility that we could be responsible for creating Universes, not just once, but repeatedly. So, I am not going to ask you to join me down that rabbit hole, dear reader. I am just going to peek into the as yet unexplained realm of the Mandela Effect.

When Nelson Mandela was reported to have died in 2013, the subject of Nelson Mandela already being dead re-surfaced, causing more and more people, to be able to share their memory of him dying much earlier than 2013. By 2013, people were able to share their information using the internet.

The original report of Nelson Mandela dying was in 1991. It was on telly, it was on the front of newspapers and it made it to mainstream media in the United Kingdom and world news.

Art Bell on his radio show in the US held a radio phone-in show, and people would call in saying they remembered Nelson Mandela dying in 1991. It was written off as a mis-memory, people believed they were confused. In 1991 there wasn't easy access to prior newspaper reports or the internet, or chat rooms and forums or blogs and YouTube channels, so it was easily dismissed.

Fast forward to 2013 and all of the above are readily available for thousands of people to be able to share their stories and their experiences, understanding the memories of events which took place surrounding Nelson Mandela's death (s). Then residue surfaced. Residue is what the Mandela Effected refer to as evidence of their prior memory.

A book surfaced that had mentioned Mandela's death in 1991, which further added to the mystery that it must have happened, there is concrete evidence, it was written in a book, it must be true. Now, it is true at that time that any facts which were published were checked and surely, if someone was mistaken about his death it would be picked up at the proof-reading stage?

Possibly not. But, for so many people to remember the first reports of Mandela's death, how could so many people have mis-remembered?

Personally, I remember Nelson Mandela dying in 1991 because I remember having conversations about it at work. My work colleagues and I were wondering, out loud, which group must have got to him in prison, and we speculated that he must have been murdered. People who experience this other set of memories, where Mandela died in 1991 are known as The Mandela Effected.

Fiona Broome was a blogger who wrote about her memory of the first funeral, and she coined the phrase, the Mandela Effect, which seems to have caught on in popularity to describe this weird experience.

Here's the thing. It is not just this one singular event in history about which people have different memories. It is not just about Nelson Mandela, dying, returning from the dead and dying again. Cynthia Larson came up with the 'Alive Again' phenomenon.

Since this information surfaced, there have been several events, mainly in and around films made in Hollywood. Hollywood actors and actresses suddenly having their names spelt differently. Famous film quotes appearing to change. Or rather, not actually change, just BE different from how the Mandela Affected remember them.

Not just people's names, but band names, song lyrics, brand names, advertising, statues, yes, statues and paintings appearing differently. With no record of any change ever having taken place. Changes in the Bible, words which people cannot remember ever reading in the Bible.

The Mandela Effected online community are a group of people, previously unconnected in any way, except now, they have a set of memories which are incorrect in this timeline, this reality, and yet their memories are the same. They have the same 'wrong' memories.

There are many theories as to how/why the Mandela Effect arose.

Initial suspicions centered around the Hadron Collider at CERN in Switzerland, with distrust reigning supreme. Those cloak and dagger scientists have collided something at a Quantum level.

The Large Hadron Collider (LHC) is a particle accelerator located at the European Council for Nuclear Research near Geneva, Switzerland. It is the world's largest and most powerful particle collider and has been instrumental in advancing our understanding of particle physics.

For some conspiracy theorrists/bewildered humans, they believe that this has collapsed our old Universe which has dispersed into the closest parallel universe, our timeline has vanished, and our consciousness has shifted over to this new reality.

Often Mandela Affected people refer to this reality as being a New Reality, a whole new place and level of experience which is foreign to them and feels strange. Not unlike a foreign Universe. A strange New World.

Here are some of the most recognised differences which come up for discussion in the Mandela Community which people often freak out about, argue for both experiences and try to explain. None of these mis-memories can easily be explained as cognitive dissonance by the people who are experiencing the feeling.

A bit like trying to explain déjà vu, which some people also think is like a glitch in the matrix, or a cross-over between multi-verses, and parallel universes we are all travelling through each day.

I am therefore offering these explanations before the List of Mandela Effects because I am aware there is a process which the Mandela Effected go through by way of accepting each effect.

It is very similar to the acceptance of Loss. As Kubler-Ross came up with, five stages of grief, in her work on Death and Dying, Denial, Anger, Bargaining, Letting Go and Acceptance is very fitting, as people realise their old reality, how they remember facts and events to have happened, which are no longer true in this reality, there is a sense of loss.

A loss of the facts, a loss of identity, a loss of information and a loss of people, often, especially if you are not surrounded by people who remember events the same way that you do. Who are these people who no longer have the same shared experience that you believe them to have had? Who are they? Where did they come from? Where did you come from? Where have you left the old versions of these people who would have remembered events the same way that you experienced them.

People have vanished. Ker-poof. In a puff of atoms colliding.

So, my List. Which is by no means exhaustive. A little search of google will bring up hundreds of Mandela Effect examples. I am listing the ones which I personally remember to be different.

For instance, there is no more Dolly, from Jaws. Tooth brace-wearing Dolly. She no longer has braces. Remember Jaws, from the James Bond Movie? Jaws, the villain, had metal teeth, when he first met his girlfriend Dolly, she smiled up at him and the sun glinted off her braces. In the film, if you watch it now, there are no braces on the actress.

There is residue about this mis-memory. Proving at least, that other people have mis-remembered. One advert in the US still shows a girl on a checkout offering a wide smile to the actor who played Jaws, and she has braces on her teeth. No, of course, this is not proof, but there is someone who makes adverts who was at least aware that Dolly had braces. Or maybe not, maybe the advert makers just happen to think that would have been an obvious match to make.

There are a few James Bond Mandela Effects, not that I can personally attest to, but there is also a picture on the internet of a scientist at CERN, sitting in his office, wearing a pair of signs around his neck with the words 'MANDELA' and 'JAMES BOND' written on them, whilst the scientist is looking happy with his work.

It clearly is a staged photo, the desk he is sitting at is stacked up with white A4 paper, but the existence of the image is enough to give pause for thought to anyone who is interested in any link between the Hadron Collider and the Mandela Effect. (It might even be photoshopped, how many people these days have themselves photographed holding up anything written on white paper/board?) It does look weird and it does seem strange.

Some Mandela Effects appear to only affect some people and not others. Some people remember the Berenstein Bears and others only know them as Berenstain Bears. This spelling has no history of changing. There is no record of the spelling being changed by the creators and yet hundreds of thousands of people claim to 100% remember that it was spelt with an 'e' and hundreds of thousands of others who have no recollection of that spelling.

There is 'residue' of this spelling on the internet, there is an old video case, showing the alternate spelling. Of course, this doesn't prove that those hundreds of thousands of Mandela affected are Right, note the capital R. All it does show is that at one time there was a batch of videos which were produced by someone who mis-spelt the name, or maybe they were Mandela affected and they weren't aware that the current spelling has changed.

Once you start looking into these weird sets of circumstances and facts, be prepared to have your mind spun, at least once. There are music lyrics which are different, particularly in Grease, the movie with John Travolta. Jim Carey now spells his name Jim Carrey. Sally Fields no longer has an 's' on the end. The acceptance speech which Sally Fields was famous for (arguably) was when she accepted her Oscar, saying, 'You like me, right now, you really, really like me'. Except, that isn't what she says now. Instead of gushing gratefully, in a charming and yet needy way, Sally Field is much more contained in her emotional expression. She uses calmer words, entirely different words.

The strange thing about Sally Fields being affected, is that her brother works for CERN. The conspiracy and mystery triggered by this little fact is evident all over YouTube and the internet.

There are verses in the Bible which have always been one way and are now different. The Bible used to have a verse where the Lion would lay down with the lamb. This now reads the Wolf will lay down with the lamb.

The phrase "the wolf lies down with eh lamb" is a common paraphrase of a biblical verse that comes from Isaiah 11:6. This verse is often used to symbolise the idea of peace, harmony, and the eventual reconciliation of opposing forces in a peaceful, ideal world.

The Lord's prayer now has words about debtors and forgiving our debt. I do not remember that one. These are explained away, as different versions of the Bible having different words. Which could be a simple explanation. The mystery is that so many people had the same gap in their education. Maybe the gap that led them to believing all versions of the Bible are the same.

If you are not Mandela Effected and none of these old memories mean anything to you, well done, give yourself a pat on the back. If you do not wish to even wonder what the rest of us are going on about, close this book now and never think of the Mandela Effect again. But, the fact you have got this far, it is worth a little voyage of discovery to uncover one of the weirdest events in the 21st century.

One of the biggest Mandela Effects for me, is one of the lines in Star Wars: Episode V – The Empire Strikes Back (1980) the movie. The character, Darth Vadar, portrayed by David Prowse and voiced by James Earl Jones, says:

'No, I am your Father' to Luke Skywalker, played by Mark Hamill, during their confrontation in Cloud City.

This isn't how I remember it. I remember Darth Vadar shouting:

'Luke, I am your father'

If you watch the movie today, he doesn't say those words.

There is a clip doing the rounds on the internet which shows the actor who played Darth Vadar, re-living the moment he said those iconic words

He says, 'Luke, I am your father' and the television presenter had to correct him. 'No, those aren't the words, the words are No, I am your father'. It was news to the actor that the words were different.

Also, I remember Pikachu, the pokemon, having a black tail., not anymore. The banker from the Monopoly Board Game used to have an eye monocle. No longer. Let's not even examine whether Mickey Mouse had braces. Or Curious George had a tail (he didn't).

Forrest Gump has been touched. Only slightly though, and since the Effect has been picked over on the internet, there seems to be an explanation. Forrest used to say 'Momma said life is like a box of chocolates, you never know what you are going to get' and now he says 'Life **was** like a box of chocolates, you never know what you are going to get'. Which doesn't really make a lot of sense. The explanation is that Forrest says both sentences, one in the movie and one in the advert/trailer for the film. Or, at different parts of the film, he uses slightly different phrasing.

The Queen song, WE ARE THE CHAMPIONS.... OF THE WORLD. Go on, sing it in your head. Now pop over to YouTube and check out the song. There is no 'OF THE WORLD' at the end. Despite many celebrities being confused about this. See James Corden and his Carpool Karaoke where he desperately searches on his music machine for the final line, which never happens. Not how I remember it.

The words to Annie have changed. There are so many Mandela Effects I haven't got room for them all in this book. Plus, a lot of them are American and I don't really have a memory about a lot of them.

The Mandela Effected community online have reported similarities in their feelings surrounding the Effect. There is a surreal, unreal feeling as you come to terms with the idea that you may have remembered history wrong. Then there is a sense of loss as you realise it is not a mis-memory, and you have joined the hundreds of thousands of other people who all remember it as you do.

Once you have come to terms with the confusion, the dismay and general unhappiness which comes from losing loved characters from your childhood, and from knowing that the timeline you remember, is nowhere near you, you then have to explain to your family members what you believe.

Generally, people who have no memory of anything remotely different to this current reality, tend not to want to get involved in any facts which can no longer be proved, and pretty much you will find yourself on your own. Please know, that you are not alone. There is an online community on hand to chew the fat with.

Every day new Mandela Effects are added as people realise how much is different. Of course, the more attention you pay to the changes, the more the changes show up!

One of the latest ones which I have paid attention to is the Mike Tyson fight where he bit off a chunk of Evander Holyfield's ear. Except that in this reality, he didn't. The fight isn't how I remembered it, at all.

In this version of reality, Tyson is warned a couple of times for nipping Holyfield's ear and the fight was stopped. In the reality I remember, Tyson sunk his teeth into Evander Holyfield's ear, bit down, and tore his head away, spitting a lump of Holyfield's ear onto the boxing mat.

I have seen a television interview with Holyfield where he is asked about the ear bite from Tyson and Holyfield showed his ear which does not appear to have much damage. It looked like it had been nipped, that or he has undergone extensive ear reconstruction surgery, it doesn't look as though anyone has taken a chomp out of it.

Another strange thing that happens with the Mandela Effect, is known as flip-flopping. One week you can look up the Ford logo and find it has a little squirly pigtail on the F, and it has always been there. The next week, you can look it up and it isn't there, never has been there, the F is totally straight. The following week you check again, and voila, the pigtail has returned. This is known as flip-flopping.

I don't think the Universe is flip-flopping around us. I don't think the Government have sent back time travellers to change our reality. I don't think anything is changing in the external, in this reality. I think we are moving through different dimensions and experiencing different realities during our one lifetime. I could be wrong. But this is the theory which makes the most sense to me.

Once you start noticing these changes, you, and this is very much a personal choice, and only you, must decide what you do with this information. It is very easy to accept a change of memory, accept you were mistaken, shake your head and voila, the new information becomes the Reality. It now forms part of Your Truth.

One of the strangest elements of this phenomenon for me, personally, is how easily people accept their own mis-memory. Generally, people are happy to think they must have been mistaken in their own information, 'Oh yes' they often say 'Now I come to think of it, you are right' and just like that, they remember it, the New Way.

For people who don't want to explore the possibility that something might be going on outside their level of understanding, it may be easier to write the phenomenon off as mis- memory, cognitive dissonance or mis-reporting, for people who are experiencing a different set of memories to this reality or timeline, it can feel extremely disconcerting.

Most of the Mandela Effect is explained away as General Ignorance, by people who cannot or do not want to, open their minds to the possibility, no matter how slight, that we are evolving as a human race, into beings who are having access to further dimensions, and quite possibly, other multiverses. We can have more than one memory about an event. There is more than one possible outcome, and depending on our own vibrational positioning, we can experience more than one reality at a time.

I think we can move through realities from one moment to the next and back again, but not experience two at once. But this is guesswork. Some people think this is what déjà vu is, we have just crossed over into another dimension where that one little incident hasn't happened yet, so we experience it for what feels like a second time.

There doesn't appear to be any explanation as to why hundreds of thousands of people would not only have an incorrect memory of an event, but they mis-remember it in the same way. Neither is there any explanation as to why not everyone is affected.

Some people remember all the MEs, other people are only affected by one or two. It may be that it is easier to deny any changes rather than try and find an explanation. Where do the old memories go? For the Mandela Effected, the old memories don't go anywhere, they remain as part of a fixed belief system to be argued for, fought over and feel distressed about.

Could it be that we are multi-dimensional beings, capable of experiencing many dimensions in one lifetime. I suspect this could be the case. As we do live in a multi-verse with many parallel universes, dimensions very similar to our own, as we ascend and change, our vibrations shift. Who knows how often we shift between dimensions.

A word of warning about discussing the Mandela Effect with your relatives, loved ones or friends. If you are affected and they aren't, they may look at you with an element of distrust, disbelief, disappointment and doubt. They may even question your sanity. Your relationships may also suffer when you realise you could be surrounded by people who are close-minded, one dimensional, non-believing Universe dwellers.

If you google or YouTube the Unaffected Mandela

Effect, you will see the reactions of people who are confronted with a reality which has altered according to a whole group of people, and yet the unaffected are not interested in hearing the information. They switch off, they change the subject, they gloss over the conversation, almost as if the information does not compute, therefore they don't want to hear it.

They generally disregard any changes they are shown, firstly, by rapidly accepting the reality they are shown, secondly, they easily dismiss their own incorrect memory and lastly, they don't want to discuss it or think about any possible disconnect or even acknowledge there is anything strange about this experience. They put it all down to a mis-memory. They accept the New Way as the way it has always been, and they don't delve into why anyone (millions of other people) may still be thinking something different.

If you are Mandela Effected, know that you are not alone.

Simulated Reality

We could be living in a simulated reality. It is one conclusion that people come to. I am not sure that it helps to think that nothing we do matters, or that we have about as much free will as a Sim. But surely we cannot ignore the pace at which AI is growing and evolving. I have a feeling that it will be AI that figures out what we are doing here and the meaning of our Universe as we know it.

In the meantime, while we wait for AI to improve itself beyond our human comprehension, we will carry on evolving and learning from each other, one way we do this is to share our stories with each other. It is a very human thing to do. We share our strange experiences, the most baffling, the most comforting, the heart-wrenching, the gut-wrenching and we grow.

Dear Reader,

Please take this little collection of experiences and do with it what you will.

It is my contribution to helping other people on their life journey.

Using synchronicity and coincidence to serve as a reminder from Spirit that you are not on your own and everything does matter.

Lots of love

Tamasin x

Bibliography and references

References in Introduction

Esther Hicks www.abraham-hicks.com

Instagram @taztasticsilver

References in Chapter I

Who, What, Where, When and How

Esther Hicks www.abraham-hicks.co

King James Version of *The Bible* Matthew 7:6

Carroll, L. (1865) *Alice's Adventures in Wonderland.* London: Macmillan.

Deepak Chopra:

https://en.wikipedia.org/wiki/Deepak_Chopra

Church Explosion story:

https://www.snopes.com/fact-check/choir-non-quorum/

Wayne Dyer:

https://en.wikipedia.org/wiki/Wayne_Dyer

Deike Begg, (2001) *Synchronicity (p.132), The Promise of Coincidence,* Thorsons

Violet Jessop Survivor of three shipwrecks story:

https://en.wikipedia.org/wiki/Violet_Jessop

Cyclist escaping death story:

https://abvnews.go.com/International/dutch-cyclist-missed-doomed-malaysia-flights-feels-lucky/story?id=24652064

Jung,C.G. (1955) *Synchronicitry, An Acausal Connecting Principle,* England, Routledge

Falling baby story:

Time Magazine, Miscellany (Oct.17. 1938)

References in Chapter II

Categories of Coincidence

Category 1 (Psychic Phenomenon)

www.tamasinblake.com

Jung, C.G.(1955), *Synchronicity, An Acausal Connecting Principl,* England, Routledge

Terence McKenna for audio recordings of Terence talking I can only signpost you to YouTube where there are half a dozen channels dedicated purely to Terence.

Cat Predicting deaths story: Oscar (therapy cat) see Wikipedia. Oscar c.2005 – 02-22-2022. Seems like a good date to die. Go Oscar!

Mark Twain death prediction:

www.documentarytube.com/articles/mark-twain-and-the-halley-s-comet-writer-predicting-own-death.

https://psychologytoday.com/us/blog.connecting-coincidence/202011/the-scarab-jung-created-coincidence-within-coincidence.

Radin, D (For further reading see: Gotspi.org Online Games)

Robertson, M. (1898) *The Wreck of the Titan.* F. Tennyson Neely

https://en.wikipedia.org/wiki/The_Wreck_of_the_Titan:_Or,_Futility

Category 2 (Life Events)

www.abraham-hicks.com

Gordon-Levitt, J. (2011) *The Tiny Book of Tiny Stories, Vol. 1,* USA, Harper Collins.

Grout, P. (2014) E3 UK Hayhouse UK Ltd

Category 3 (Nature)

Burroughs, J (April 3, 1837 – March 29, 1921)

www.cainer.com Cainer Astrology Site

Sams,G. (2009) *Sun of God,* Red Wheel, Weiser, LLC

Category 4 (Animals)

Webster's Dictionary: www.merriam-webster.com/dictionary/totem

Category 5 (People)

Laura Buxton story:

https://www.snopes.com/fact-check/whether-balloon/

Deepak Chopra:

https://en.wikipedia.org/wiki/Deepak_Chopra

https://www.Twinstrangers.net

Category 7 (Inanimate Objects)

www.abraham0hicks

Wayne Dyer – Take Control of Your Attitude/ Wayne Dyer Meditation. You tube channel @ Genius Mindset

L. Frank Baum's coat story (the Wizard of Oz):

https://www.snopes.com/fact-check/coat-of-baums/

Category 8 (Spiritual)

Stuart Chase (March 9,1888- November 16 1985) was an American economist, social theorist and writer.

Nathanson, B.N, M.D. (1996) *Hand of God*, a journey from Death to Life by the abortion doctor who changed his mind, US Regenery Publishing Inc.

Nope (2022) film directed by Jordan Peele.

A Wild Women's Soul on Facebook.

Category 9 (Data)

"Dancing Queen" (Andersson, Ulvaeus, Anderson,1976) by Abba.

"I'd like to teach the world to sing" (Bill Backer, Billy Davis, Roger Cook, Roger Greenaway, 1971) the New Seekers.

"I'm a Celebrity – Get Me Out of Here!" (Richard Cowles, Natalka Znak, Stewart Morris, Mark Busk-Cowley, Alexander Gardiner, Jim Allen, Brent Baker 2003-2019)

Michael McIntyre's Big Show (Michael McIntyre, 2015-2016)

Unice (2017), *Sun Signs in Love,* Amazon Kindle

Category 10

Wayner Dyer talking about *The Tao Te Ching* & *A Million Little Pieces* can be found on Youtube @marcoangelo and probably half a dozen other channels.

www.epochconverter.com

Lee Evans:

https://en.wikipedia.org/wiki/Lee_Evans_(comedian)

Terence McKenna:

https://en.wikipedia.or/wiki/Terence_McKenna

"The number 23" (Schumacher, 2007) is a

psychological thriller starring Jim Carrey and directed by Joel Schumacher.

References in Chapter III:

Anti-Synchronicities

Edward Murphy,Jr :

https://en.wikipedia.org/wiki/Edward_A._Murphy_Jr.

References in Chapter IV:

Synchronicity Journal

Abraham-Hicks (www.abraham-hicks.com)

Articulate Board Game: Articulate (1992). Designed by Andrew Bryceson. Published by Drummon Park Ltd.

Celebrity Antiques Road Trip:

BBC.(Producer),(2021), Celebrity Antiques Road Trip (Television Series), United Kingdom:BBC.

Cannon, D. (2001). The Convoluted Universe, Huntsville, AR; Ozark Mountain Publishing.

Davies, G. (Creator). (2013-2017). Man Down (Television Series). UK: Channel 4.

Deepak Chopra:

https://en.wikipedia.org/wiki/Deepak _Chopra

Pirates of the Caribbean film franchise
Depp,J. (b.1963). Actor and Producer.

Wayne Dyer:

https://en.wikipedia.org/wiki/Wayne_Dyer

Instagram@taztasticsilver

Fear of 13 documentary:

https://www.imdb.com/title/rt5083702/

Patrick Gamble – psychic artist, creator of Oracle cards. He hosts weekend psychic art workshops:

https://www.facebook.com/events/dan-rox/patrick-gamble-spiritual-artist/557794762440286/

McBroom,A. (1977). The Rose (recorded by Bette Midler), on The Rose (Soundtrack). Los Angelees, CA: Atlantic Records.

Shinn, F.S. (1925). *The Game of Life and How to Play It*. New York, NY: Devorss & Company.

Alan Watts Youtube channel 'By Letting it go, you get the control'.

Oscar Wilde:

https://en.wikipedia.org/wiki/Oscar_Wilde.

References in Chapter V:

Symbolism Meanings

Art bell. Coast to Coast AM (1994). Hosted by Art Bell. (Radio Talk Show). Pahrump, Nevada: Premiere Networks.

Bhagavad Gita (2000), Translated by Eknath Easwaran, Tomales, CA: Nilgiri Press.

Phrase Meaning of Bobs Your Uncle: https://www.phrases.org.uk/meanings/bobs-your-uncle.html
Psychic library:

https.psychiclibrary.com/beyondBooks/penny-superstition.

Wayne Dyer: https://en.wikipedia.org/wiki/Wayne_Dyer

Author: Grose, F.(1785). Title: A Dictionary of the Vulgar Tongue. Publisher: Printed for S. Hooper.

Jung, Carl.G. (1969) *The Archetypes and the Collective Unconscious*. US, Princeton University Press. Translation by R.F.C. Hull.

References in Chapter VI:

Curiouser and Curiouser (otherwise known as Full Woo)

Art bell. Coast to Coast AM (1994). Hosted by Art Bell. (Radio Talk Show). Pahrump, Nevada: Premiere Networks.

Fiona Broom. The Mandela Effect: https://fionabroome.com/

Hadron Collider CERN: https://home.cern/science/accelerators/large-hadron-collider

"Forrest Gump" (1994). Directed by Robert Zemeckis (Film). United States: Paramount Pictures.

Esther Hicks: www.Abraham-hicks.com

Mercury,F. (1977). We are the Champions. On News of the World, performed by Queen. United Kingdom: EMI.

R.A. Moody, (1975) *Life After Life*, US, Mockingbird books.

Pikachu. (1996). (Electric-type Pokemon known for its yellow fur and lightning bolt-shaped tail). In Pokemon: The Animated Sereies (TV series), Directed by Kunihiko Yuvama, Japan: OLM,Inc.

Kubler-Ross, E. (1969). *On Death and Dying,* New York, NY: Scribner.

"The Spy Who Loved Me" (1977). Directed by Lewis Gibert. (Film), UK: Eon Productions.

Star Wars: Episode V. The Empire Strikes Back (1980). Directed by Irvin Kershner, (Film). United States: Lucasfilm Ltd.

The lion no longer lies with the lamb. Isaiah 11:6 in *The Bibl*e (KJV)

The Phrase Finder

Webster's Dictionary: www.merriam-website

Rowling, J.K:

https://en.wikipedia.org/wiki/J._K._Rowling.

https.psychiclibrary.com/beyondBooks/penny-superstition.

Wayne Dyer: https://en.wikipedia.org/wiki/Wayne_Dyer

ABOUT THE AUTHOR

Spring: 1966 -1986 A fabulously rocky start, a council house upbringing in relative poverty, born in the East End of London. Growing up mainly in Essex: Billericay, Laindon, Wickford, Southend on Sea, Westcliff on Sea.

Summer: 1986 - 2006 It was a tale of a couple of decades, self-development, single parenthood, studying for an Open University Degree. Lots of part-time jobs and adventures in making ends meet.

Autumn: 2006 – current (2023) Sticking to a path of spirituality, finding meaning in the everyday. Join my coincidental journey on Youtube @synchronicitytime (Time for Synchronicity), also my Instagram @taztasticsilver.

If you have had any unexplained experiences, please do feel free to share it with me at www.tamasinblake.com.

SYNCHRONICITIES AND COINCIDENCES IN JANUARY

SYNCHRONICITIES AND COINCIDENCES IN FEBRUARY

Tamasin F. Blake

SYNCHRONICITIES AND COINCIDENCES IN MARCH

SYNCHRONICITIES AND COINCIDENCES IN APRIL

Tamasin F. Blake

SYNCHRONICITIES AND COINCIDENCES IN MAY

SYNCHRONICITIES AND COINCIDENCES IN JUNE

Tamasin F. Blake

SYNCHRONICITIES AND COINCIDENCES IN JULY

SYNCHRONICITIES AND COINCIDENCES IN AUGUST

Tamasin F. Blake

SYNCHRONICITIES AND COINCIDENCES IN SEPTEMBER

SYNCHRONICITIES AND COINCIDENCES IN OCTOBER

Tamasin F. Blake

SYNCHRONICITIES AND COINCIDENCES IN NOVEMBER

SYNCHRONICITIES AND COINCIDENCES IN DECEMBER

Printed in Great Britain
by Amazon